GET YOUR
MESSAGE
ACROSS

Dr. John R. Diekman is assistant professor of
speech communication at St. John's University,
New York, New York.

JOHN R. DIEKMAN

GET YOUR MESSAGE ACROSS

How to improve communication

A SPECTRUM BOOK

PRENTICE-HALL, INC., Englewood Cliffs, N.J. 07632

Library of Congress Cataloging in Publication Data

Diekman, John R
  Get your message across.

  (A Spectrum Book)
  Includes index.
    1. Communication. 2. Interpersonal communica-
tion. I. Title.
  P90.D5   001.5   78-27551
  ISBN 0-13-354324-2
  ISBN 0-13-354316-1 pbk.

Editorial/production supervision and interior
    design by Norma Karlin
Cover illustration by Rudi Von Briel
Illustrations by James P. Monroe
Manufacturing buyer: Cathie Lenard

10 9 8 7 6 5 4 3 2 1

Prentice-Hall International, Inc., *London*
Prentice-Hall of Australia Pty. Limited, *Sydney*
Prentice-Hall of Canada, Ltd., *Toronto*
Prentice-Hall of India Private Limited, *New Delhi*
Prentice-Hall of Japan, Inc., *Tokyo*
Prentice-Hall of Southeast Asia Pte. Ltd., *Singapore*
Whitehall Books Limited, *Wellington, New Zealand*

For my family

Contents

INTRODUCTION
Learning about Communication, 3

**EFFECTIVE
COMMUNICATION**
A Model of the Communication Process, 11

Human Communication:
Beyond the Model to the Reality, 25

Effective Communication:
How to Make It Happen, 35

THE TRANSITION
Putting Communication to Work, 51

AUTHENTIC COMMUNICATION
Getting It All Together, 55
The Question of Communion: A Beginning, 57
Understanding the Self, 61
Coming into Your Own as a Communicator, 89
The Experiences of Human Communication, 99

AFTERWORD
Final Thoughts, 123
Index, 129

GET YOUR
MESSAGE
ACROSS

INTRODUCTION

Learning
about communication

Think for a moment about your communication today. Maybe focus on one specific exchange: with your husband or a neighbor or a friend. How did it go? How would you rate the interaction? Was anything constructive accomplished, or was it an exercise in futility? If you are like most people, you would probably have to admit that many of your relationships are plagued by misunderstandings, disagreements, frustrations, and tensions—all of which you may attribute to breakdowns in communication.

When we have a hard time getting along with someone else, when another person disagrees with us, when a friend refuses to do what we want—these are some of the times when we are likely to put the blame on a breakdown in communication. But I am not at all convinced that this scapegoating is an accurate assessment of what is really happening. **There is an important difference between** *communication* **and** *communication effectiveness.*

Communication. In the most fundamental sense of the word, "communication" refers to the sending and receiving of messages, both verbal and nonverbal. When considered in this way, it is clear that communication never really breaks down. It is happening all the time; we are forever exchanging all kinds of messages with other people, even in our silence. (In fact, a silent moment may be one in which the message-sending is *most* obvious.)

Communication effectiveness. Effective communication is another matter altogether. Even the most superficial look at the problems with people in our day-to-day living reveals that communication effectiveness breaks down all the time. Here is a simple example of what I mean:

Mrs. D. is a 52-year-old woman. By her own definition, she is conservative in her attitudes and beliefs. Her 16-year-old daughter, Beth, comes home from school one afternoon and announces that she and her boyfriend are now going steady. Mrs. D. hits the roof and says, in effect, "I forbid it!" Beth becomes defensive—then defiant—and responds, "Why?" (Sound familiar, Mom?) And so it begins. Tempers flare. Voices are raised. There is a long litany of accusations and counter-accusations. In sum, a disaster. It ends, predictably, with Mrs. D. calling Beth a tramp and with Beth running from the house, slamming the door behind her.

What has happened here? Certainly there has not been a breakdown in communication. In fact, a great deal has been communicated. A lot has been said. And it probably will be remembered for some time to come. But the communication effectiveness *has* broken down. Words were spoken in anger and frustration. The discussion became a fight, with bitterness and resentment the inevitable results. Communicating is not really the problem; we are always communicating, in the sense that we are continually sending and receiving messages. These messages are not always spoken, but they are there nonetheless. Beth's storming out of the house—without saying a word—spoke a wealth of information. But communicating *effectively*—communicating in a productive, helping, healing way—that is the problem. How do we make it happen? How do we do it? These are the important questions. And answering these questions, and making your communication more effective in the process, is what this book is all about.

The book itself is divided into two main sections: *Effective Communication* and *Authentic Communication*. The first main section has several purposes:

1. To make you aware of how the process of communication works.
2. To make you aware of the effect of perception on your communication behavior.
3. To make you aware of a number of things you can do to make your communication more effective. (These tips are easily applied and absolutely guaranteed, incidentally!)
4. To make you aware of how important *listening* is to effective communication. (Here, too, there are some surefire ways to make yourself a better listener.)

The second main section of the book aims at helping you to grow up in an emotional way, so that your relationships can be more intimate and helping. We all grow up in a physical way; that is rarely a problem. We get bigger and older and, eventually, grayer. But not all of us grow up in an emotional way. Not by a long shot. And it is a simple fact of life that emotional children—people who have *not* grown up emotionally—will *never* be able to carry off a meaningful relationship, in or out of marriage.

Many of us who have grown up physically continue to play the emotional games of our childhood; we meet one another with our defenses up and our social masks firmly in place. The inevitable result is a communication experience that is shallow and unsatisfying. But I am getting ahead of myself. For the moment, let's just say that growing up is what this second main section is about. More specifically, its purposes are as follows:

1. To make you aware of your own growth potential and to move you in the direction of increased personal growth.

2. To make you aware of who you are in relation to other people.

3. To make you critically aware of the quality and character of your own interpersonal relationships.

4. To make you aware of what you can do to enhance the quality of those relationships.

Interspersed throughout the book are a number of *Awareness* principles. These are brief insights that will focus your attention on some of the many facets of our interpersonal experiences. In most cases, these *Awareness* principles complement the material in the text; but they are *not* summaries. Each is a self-contained unit—a stimulus to make you pause and reflect on the effectiveness of your own communication behavior.

There are also several sections titled *Things to Do*. In each of these sections you will find some suggestions for things you can do to make what you have learned a part of your pattern of everyday behavior.

All of this is by way of introduction. Now it is time to begin. Even as I write this, I find myself learning more about what makes effective communication happen. And so we can learn from one another. I appreciate the chance to share this experience with you.

EFFECTIVE COMMUNICATION

A model of the communication process

Communication is an ongoing process of interaction between people, people interacting in social situations. This is the experience of human communication. Messages are only the things we communicate. The message—any message—standing by itself is not a communication at all, but simply a string of words. These messages can be rightly understood only insofar as they are given expression by people and are heard by other people. What we are saying here is that the message must be considered "in relief"—in the context of the reality of people speaking with one another.

Communication is a people-process, and the study of interpersonal communication allows us to understand the human dynamics of that process. Because the process is con-

tinuous and ongoing, it is impossible to capture that process
totally in a single pictorial diagram or model. And yet, recognizing its limitations, we can suggest a model that reflects
the thrust and direction of the communication process. Such
a model is helpful because it allows us to study the various
elements that work together to make communication happen. The model is a means to the end of becoming more
critically aware of the tremendous complexity of human
communication.

Let us construct a model of the communication process.
Because communication is a people-process, we would do
well to begin by putting people in touch with one another, as
shown in Figure 1. We can now begin to see some of the basic
elements of the communication event:

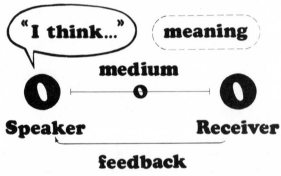

Figure 1

1. There is a *speaker* who has an idea he wishes to share
with someone else. He packages that idea in words and for-
mulates his *message*.

2. There is a *receiver* who picks up on that idea by as-
similating the message. This is the point at which the receiver
of the message gives that message a certain *meaning*. Remember that the message—in and of itself—really has no
meaning. **Meaning is in people, *not* words**. In practical

terms, it makes no difference what meaning the *speaker* has in mind when he packages his message. What *counts* is the meaning the *receiver* gives that message. The receiver responds to the meaning in his own mind, not necessarily to the meaning in the mind of the speaker. Understanding this reality is central to making your communication more effective. In my classroom teaching, I stress this point with the phrase: **The message *is* the message received**. You are responding to what you *hear* me say—and that is not necessarily what I am *intending* to say.

3. There is a *medium*—the means by which the message is transmitted. This medium can be very nearly anything: a spoken word, television, newspaper, and so on. The medium for the message can also be nonverbal or unspoken: the tone of voice or its volume, a wave of the hand, a shrug of the shoulders, a certain style of dress—all of these things speak messages just as surely as any spoken or written word.

4. There is a *feedback loop* that charts the response from the receiver back to the speaker. Feedback is a kind of reciprocal message, one that is sent as a reply to the original message. The feedback loop reminds us that we are dealing with a dynamic, ongoing process. Communication is a back-and-forth experience, a matter of give-and-take between persons.

AWARENESS 1

Communication is a people-process. And effective communication is simply good "people relations." It's not a matter of technique or gimmicks; it is a matter of sensitivity and understanding and responsiveness. It's hard work. But you *can* be effective if you really want to be. And if you work at it.

What it really comes down to is this: If you respect yourself and are striving to become all the person you can be, then you will be effective as you speak with others. And if you respect others and genuinely want to let them into your life, then you will be effective as you listen to others. **Communication is people sharing themselves with one another. The better you are at sharing, the better you will be at communicating.**

The model shown in Figure 1 is simple enough. It indicates the elements that make up any communication transaction. But at this point the model is incomplete and, therefore, misleading. It is *too* simple. It needs elaboration in order to make it an accurate reflection of the real-life workings of the communication process. And so we have to go back to work on it.

First of all, there is a problem with the words *speaker* and *receiver*. These designations are abstractions. I have yet to see a *speaker* or a *receiver* communicating. **Only people communicate, real-life people.** And so we have to put real people into our model. We can do this by referring to the participants in the process as *I* and *The Other*. These new designations remind us that communication is something that happens between individual persons—absolutely unique persons with their own individual ways of looking at themselves, other people, and the world.

These new designations also remind us that each person—actively involved in the communication process—is both sending and receiving messages continually. Even as I am speaking to you, for example, you are giving me feedback. You are speaking back all the while, even before you verbalize your response: You may be moving closer to me or backing away from me; you may be smiling or frowning; nodding your head, "yes," or shaking your head, "no"; listening intently or yawning with boredom and disinterest. And I am aware of all this and am programming it in my own head,

14

even as I continue to speak. In other words, I am speaking my message and yet receiving a number of messages from you at the same time. You, on the other hand, are receiving my messages and yet sending your own messages at the same time. Our model will clearly reflect this cyclical dimension of the communication process if we add what might be called a *feedforward loop*, as shown in Figure 2.

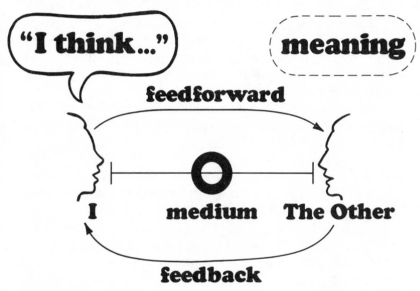

Figure 2

To talk in terms of a *speaker* and a *receiver* makes the model too static and fixed to be an accurate reflection of the dynamic process of human communication. The designations of *I* and *The Other* help to instill that sense of the dynamic. But we need still more. The model must clearly point out the absolute uniqueness of the persons involved in the communication event. We can accomplish this by enclosing the *I* and *The Other* in their own *life-worlds*.

Each of us inhabits a certain amount of physical space;

we take up a certain amount of room in the physical world. But we also take up a certain amount of psychic or emotional space. That is, we each have our own unique thoughts, feelings, values, attitudes, prejudices, biases, experiences, and perceptions. These are the things that make up your life-world. And every message you receive is *filtered* through your life-world. Your thoughts and feelings and values and attitudes and prejudices and biases and experiences and perceptions all affect the way in which you "hear" any message. And, of course, they affect your response to that message. Remember: The message *is* the message received. What counts in the communication transaction is the way in which you receive my message, because this is the thing to which you are responding. What you *hear* me saying is more important than what I *mean* to say. And your life-world plays an important role in your reception of my message.

We will recount the importance of the life-world later on, especially as we consider the *perceptual process*. For the moment, know what the life-world is and what it does by way of determining your reception of my message. And let us include it in our model, as shown in Figure 3.

Now we are beginning to get somewhere. But we still have some work to do. There is still something lacking in the model—namely, a *context*. Human communication never takes place in a vacuum. There is always a situation, always a setting for the interaction. And understanding this setting is critical to our understanding of the interaction itself, because the situation affects the workings of the interaction in a profound way. **You behave differently from one situation to the next, not only because the people with whom you are interacting may change, but also because of the change in setting itself.** You communicate in a certain way at home, for example, and in quite another way at work. The setting in which you find yourself "speaks" to you. And you get the message. You respond in a way that is appropriate to where you are. We can appreciate the importance of the setting by

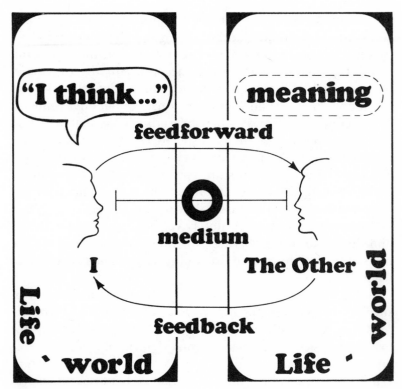

Figure 3

remembering that so-called "antisocial" behavior is always considered such because it is inappropriate *at a given time* and *in a given place*.

We can refer to the context-dimension of the model as the *social environment*. This designation is a handy one because it reminds us that in any relationship and every communication there is an *ecological question* with which we will have to be concerned: **We must maintain a *balance* between ourselves as communicators and the social environment within which we do that communicating**. Not only does the environment of the communication affect the transaction; the transaction (how it works itself out and what we do with one another) has a significant counter-effect on the environment. This unique kind of dialogue—the back-and-forth that takes place between the environment and the communication that takes place therein—accounts for the phenomenon of social change. For example, you behave in school—as a student—in a certain way in response to that environment: You follow certain prescribed procedures for matriculation and registration; you pursue a specified course of study; you meet guidelines for classroom behavior and deadlines when assignments are due; in sum, you perform your role in accordance with the environment in which you find yourself. This particular environment has an impact on you which other environments may not have. You say certain things and do certain things because of where you are; and you do not say certain things and do not do certain things because of where you are.

But you have an impact on your environment just as surely as it has an impact on you. The way in which you perform your behaviors—in your role as a student, for example—goes a long way toward determining the kind of environment your school maintains. In a curious (but very real) way, you *are* the school. It can be no better as an institution than you are as a member of that institution.

Precisely the same thing happens in any other communication situation. When you finish school and land a permanent job, you experience the same thing. In any job setting there is an established climate or environment. You will sense this and, before long, will get a feeling for the place. In other words, you will discern what your role in the organization is and what behaviors you will have to perform in order to fill that role. You may receive a job description from the personnel manager, and this will spell out what is expected of you. You will also receive input about your role from your immediate supervisor and your fellow employees. But all the while *you* will be filling that position *in your own unique way.* You will be working in response to your environment, and, at the same time, the way you handle your role will serve to reshape that environment.

One of the purposes of this book is to make you more aware of yourself as a communicator so that you will be able to work on your environment in a positive way, so that you will be able to make significant contributions to whatever situation in which you find yourself. My own experience as a communication consultant for businesses is that most organizational problems are not related to the business operation itself. Most employees know their jobs; the problems they have are "people problems"—getting along, cooperating on a given project, and so on. This book should help you to cope with such interpersonal problems.

Let's look at one final example: You are born into a certain role in your family—a son or a daughter in relation to your parents, a brother or a sister in relation to your brothers and sisters. Each member of the family performs certain behaviors in response to these roles. Your parents provide for your well-being, for example, and you do chores around the house. These and other behaviors are demanded because the environment is a home. But the way in which these various role-behaviors are performed determines the *environmental quality* of the home. Again we have an ecological question: Is the atmosphere in the home helpful or detrimental? Is it a nourishing or a toxic place in which to live?

This question of the ecology of relationships is extremely important to our appreciation and understanding of the process of interpersonal communication. The environment in which you find yourself has an effect on you. But you have a tremendous effect on it as well. **Human relationships are fragile things, and they must be cared for.** This is still another reason why we must develop a critical sense of who we are *in relation* to other people.

Well then, we now have a workable model of the human

communication process. The model is *descriptive*, inasmuch as it reveals the structure of a given communication event. It is also *prescriptive*, in that it pinpoints factors we have to be aware of and pitfalls we must guard against. Our finished model is shown in Figure 4.

Figure 4

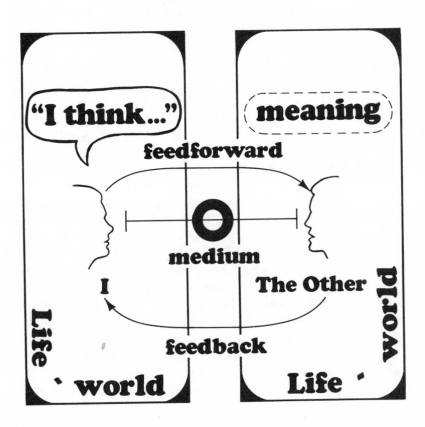

Things to Do

1. Let me say it again, because it is critical: **The message** *is* **the message received**. It does not really matter what I have in mind when I speak my message; you are responding not to what I *mean* to say but to what you *hear* me say. Now the question is how to make this insight work for me? And the answer is simple enough: *I always have to double-check my message*. I have to ask what you *heard* me say. Otherwise we might be talking (and maybe fighting) about two completely different things. How many times—after an argument—do we say, "But that's not what I meant!"? The problem with such a disclaimer is that by then it is too late; the damage has been done.

Try it. Right now. Today. See if you can't make it work for yourself. And, of course, have your partner do the same thing. Make sure that each of you knows exactly what the other has meant to say. And only *then* respond. *Now* you're talking!

2. We understand now that the various elements that make up our life-world can work to distort the messages we hear. But what do we do to minimize that distortion? What can we do to prevent this from hindering our communication effectiveness? I am assuming here that forewarned is forearmed; that an awareness of what is happening will serve to make us more cautious (and therefore more effective). What you do here is simply to get in touch with your own life-world, to take it apart and examine its components. It is a matter of introspective self-awareness, pure and simple. This introspection is often painful, because you may not like what you see. But it is absolutely necessary to your communication effectiveness. Let me suggest some questions that might serve as a starting-point for this introspective process:

What am I thinking and feeling at this very minute? What about what I want? Am I trying to force something, when it might not be happening of its own accord? If so, am I pressing (trying too hard to put my best foot forward) in my relationships?

What about my prejudgments and biases? Am I meeting other people not as individuals, but as stereotyped preconceptions? If so, then I am losing a great deal, because I am not meeting them at all. Do I *expect* people of racial or ethnic backgrounds different from my own to behave in a certain way? Am I looking for these behaviors and perhaps misinterpreting what they mean?

What about where I come from? Where I grew up? This surely has a bearing on how I see the world. And so I need to get in touch with those life-experiences that shape my perceptions of things.

There are many more questions we need to ask of ourselves. These are just a few. They can help you to tune into *who you are* as a person, and to recognize how your perceptions of realities affect your behavior.

3. It is almost considered chic nowadays for couples who break up to say that they had to part in order to keep growing as individuals. Well, self-growth is certainly the goal for which we all should be striving. But that growth can be a mutual thing. It is possible for two people to keep growing and to remain together at the same time. It seems to me that preserving the relationship is a matter of learning to accommodate *change*. All living is change; it is an inevitable part of our life-experience. But too few of us know how to cope with change, so change puts a real strain on many relationships. Here are some things you can do to help cope with change and, thereby, enhance the quality of your relationships:

- *Expect change. Welcome it. Seek it out.* Your tastes, your values, your preferences—you yourself—are in a constant process of evolution. Do not be afraid of changes. The only time you stop changing is when you are dead.

- *Tune into the changes taking place within you.* Try keeping a running journal of your feelings: "This is how I feel about. . . ." Date your entries and check them over regularly to chart your changes. You keep track of the pounds you gain and lose; you religiously count the gray hairs; why not keep a record of the things that are most truly you—your feelings?

- *Share your changes with your partner.* Keeping a relationship going is a matter of two people trying to keep up with one another. We begin by recognizing the inevitability of changes in one another. And then we share those changes, always letting the other person know where we are emotionally. You can only know me when I tell you who I am. And that means I must tell you what I am feeling.

Human communication: beyond the model to the reality

The model we developed (Figure 4) is a major step in our attempt to come to terms with the experience of interpersonal communication. But the model—any model of anything—is not the reality it mirrors. It is an abstraction of that reality. Now we must turn our attention to the human reality of people communicating with one another. We have to pose some basic questions in regard to the communication experience:

What is happening?
How is it happening?
Why is it happening as it is?

In any communication situation, in order to understand *what* is happening—and *how*—and, perhaps most important of all, *why*—it is necessary to appreciate the significance of the following assertion: **Communication is largely a matter of perception.** The messages we exchange with one another in any interpersonal transaction have no meaning in and of themselves. At least the *words* that make up the messages have no meaning standing alone. These words—and the messages they constitute—only take on meaning when the communicators assign them a meaning. And this assigning of meaning is what perception is all about.

PERCEPTION

We are constantly being bombarded by stimuli of every imaginable sort. Take a moment and consider the stimuli that are forcing themselves on your consciousness at this very instant. Look around you. And listen. And smell. And touch. Let all your senses speak to you. Your senses, after all, are serving as go-betweens for these stimuli. The size of the room you are in, the color of the walls, the feel of the chair in which you are sitting, the sounds of the children playing just outside the window, the music on the stereo, the dampness in the air—all these stimuli and many more may be bombarding you at this very moment. But you are not a passive receptacle for these stimuli. Your central nervous system is sorting through all these sensations and programming them in such a way that they fit together in a coherent pattern. You are able to put these stimuli in some kind of perspective, thereby allowing you to understand the things happening around you. In other words, you are an active participant in the perceptual process. *Perception is something you do.*

By paying close attention to your own perceptual patterns, you will discover that you piece together these patterns in your own unique, individual way. You and I can experience the same concrete reality, but *perceive* that reality in two completely different ways. Such perceptual differences can only be explained by understanding that we are not blank tablets on which the world "out there" writes its meanings. On the contrary. **Meaning is something we impose on our environment. We interject our entire selves into the perceptual process.**

Perception is an active enterprise; it is something we *do*. This accounts for the fact that you and I can "see" the same film at the same time under the same circumstances and yet perceive the film in two different ways. You think that it is a great film; I find it a bore. Who is right? What *is* the film— good or bad? Well, the film *is* whatever we perceive it to be. It is futile for us to argue about the merits of the film unless we are both aware of the undeniable fact that we are not arguing about the film at all, but rather, about our *perceptions* of the film.

Not only is perception an *active enterprise*; it is also a *selective event*. That is, we actually select that which we perceive and the way in which we perceive it. We organize sensory stimuli, sort through them, and assimilate them in such a way that we construct a meaningful picture of the world— *our own unique picture of that world*. Often we do this in a prereflective way; without conscious thought. But we do it nonetheless. In a very real sense, we create the world we see. Our communication, then, is a way of relating to that world. If we want to understand our messages better, we must first understand the way in which we piece together our vision of reality, and there are several factors involved in this selective perception:

Physiological Determinants

Each of us has certain physiological strengths and weaknesses; we are not all built the same way. If a student is nearsighted, for example, and is seated at the back of the classroom, he will not be able to perceive the significance of the professor's writing on the blackboard. He simply will not be able to make it out, and thus it is not a part of his *perceptual field*. It will have no meaning for him.

Psychological Predisposition

Each of us has certain needs, fears, frustrations, anxieties, ambitions, and ideals—the sum total of which is the individual's life-world. All of these things have a definite impact on the way in which another person or an event is perceived. The person who maintains a deep-seated insecurity about his own worth, for example, may distort the most innocent of remarks and perceive it as a direct attack upon himself as a person.

Career Orientation and Interests

Each of us has a background of training and experience that causes us to look for certain things in a given situation. Imagine, for example, an automobile accident on the highway. An off-duty policeman, a physician, and a priest happen by the accident scene and stop to render assistance. The policeman will remove the injured parties from the wreckage and then reroute traffic away from the area. The physician will begin the process of caring for the injured, providing whatever assistance he can under the emergency circumstances. The priest will comfort the uninjured persons and provide for the spiritual well-being of the injured parties. Afterward, the policeman may report that one of the drivers had been speeding and was responsible for the accident. The physician may talk about the emergency tracheotomy he had to perform. The priest may comment that one of the victims had accomplished a spiritual reconciliation with God. The *same* event, but three *different* perceptions of that event because *the observers were looking for different things.*

Many so-called breakdowns in communication can be traced directly to different perceptions of the same event. Meaningful, productive, significant communication can only happen when there is a *shared perception.* There must be some kind of overlap between the perceptual experiences of the persons involved in the communication event if there is going to be a sharing of meaning (see Figure 5).

Shared meaning is not easy to come by, because human interaction is such a complicated affair. It has been suggested that communication between two persons would be a relatively simple thing if, in fact, there were only two persons involved. In reality, however, there are *six* participants entering into any two-person interaction (see Figure 6). It works like this:

On the one hand, we have

1. Smith as he perceives himself
2. Smith as he is perceived by Jones
3. Smith as he "really" is

On the other hand, we have

1. Jones as he perceives himself
2. Jones as he is perceived by Smith
3. Jones as he "really" is

These "other selves" can be referred to as *perceptual ghosts.* And they haunt virtually every communication situation. If the participants in the transaction do not recognize

It is at this point that the sending and receiving of messages becomes a sharing of meaning.

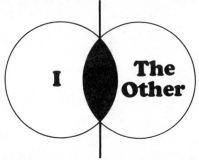

This is the moment of real communication.

Figure 5

these ghosts—if they do not get them out into the open where they can be seen and dealt with—the results can be disastrous. Here is what happens: I "am" in a certain way; I behave in a certain way because various physical, emotional, and social influences are working on me. I also "see" myself in a certain way, and the way in which I "see" myself is not necessarily the way I "am." Interaction makes things even more complicated, because you may "see" me in still another way; and the way in which you "see" me is not necessarily the way in which I "see" myself, nor the way I really "am."

Communication is a complicated matter. Little wonder,

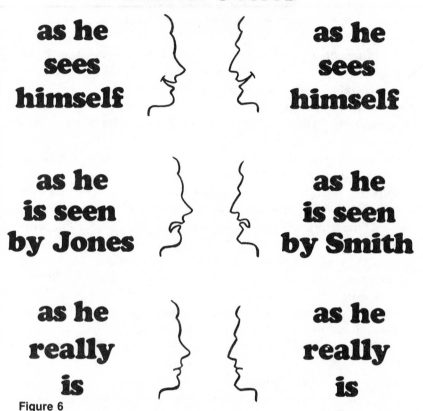

Smith Jones

as he   as he
sees   sees
himself   himself

as he   as he
is seen   is seen
by Jones   by Smith

as he   as he
really   really
is   is

Figure 6

then, that we experience difficulties in our relationships. Alice and John were a couple who—before they joined a therapy group—found themselves fighting all the time. The theme of their fighting was a familiar one: her complaints about his sloppiness around the house. That was the *subject* of their fighting. But was it the *reason* for the fights? The answer to that question has to do with the whole issue of perception.

31

A few counseling sessions revealed what was happening
in their relationship: As she saw herself, Alice simply wanted
to be proud of their home, and she got angry when John did
not cooperate in keeping it clean. John, however, saw her as
nagging and making a big fuss about nothing. After all, he
reasoned, ". . . a man's house is his castle," and he should be
comfortable and relaxed in his own home. In reality, Alice
was experiencing a great deal of frustration and anxiety,
sensing that she had locked herself into a humdrum existence that had left her feeling empty and unfulfilled. But she
did not know what to do about these feelings; she could
barely admit them to herself, much less share them openly
with John. And so she vented her pent-up feelings of frustration by focusing on John's sloppy habits.

The problem, of course, was that Alice and John were
fighting for the wrong *reason*. And so all the time and energy
they expended was wasted. The *real* issue here had nothing
to do with how the house looked. That was totally irrelevant.
The issue was what Alice was feeling. It was John's inability to
reach out to her and to speak to her needs. But he could
never have reached out to her had he not become aware of
what she needed. And that awareness could only come when
they were able to talk about what was happening to them,
individually and in their *relationship*.

It is imperative that we exorcise these perceptual ghosts
from our interpersonal transactions. And helping you to
conduct that exorcism is what this book is all about.

AWARENESS 2

The most fundamental, most basic of all perceptions is my
perception of myself—my self-image.

The power of positive thinking is often overrated. Positive
thinking—all by itself—will not accomplish anything. But it
is true that I'll be unable to accomplish anything significant

unless I proceed from a *positive self-image*. If I don't feel good about myself, I will overcompensate for my perceived inadequacy: I will become too loud, too forceful, too verbal. I will come on just a little bit too strong. Obnoxious, pushy behavior—in myself and in others—is almost always a cry for help.

Having a positive self-image does not mean that I see myself as some kind of superman. It simply means that I like myself, that I respect myself, that I trust my feelings and my judgments. **Having a positive self-image is the same thing as feeling self-worth.** And it is at the heart of all productive behavior.

Things to Do

1. Many of us spend considerable amounts of time feeling angry. When someone disagrees with us, we become livid: "How could anyone be so stupid?," we wonder. Well, the next time that you feel this anger swelling up inside you, recite this little formula: **As the other person sees it, he is right**. We *all* have our own unique individual perceptions of reality.

Most of our arguments are pointless, in that they rarely come to any positive end. The more we argue—and the louder—the more adamant we become about our respective perceptions. Instead of arguing about a certain issue, simply *discuss* it. Share your viewpoints (another word for perceptions) with one another, maybe even try to persuade one another. But *let it go* at that. Remember that for the other person to disagree with you does *not* diminish you as a person; it does not mean that you are wrong. It is simply a difference of opinion.

2. We really do construct the world in which we live. What you see *is* what you get. It's all a matter of vision. Many

people are myopic in the vision they have of themselves and their potential for growth. And this kind of nearsightedness makes their lives drudgery, not adventure. They really don't like themselves and—because they don't think much of themselves—they resent the accomplishments, success, and happiness of others. They become narrow-minded, petty, mean, miserable. The person without vision is an emotional Neanderthal; he's still a caveman. He sits on the stoop with his half-warm can of beer, waiting for the ball game on TV. He is oblivious to all the splendid growth-possibilities around him. He is just *existing*, not really *living*.

Some questions to ask of myself:

What about my own vision? Am I tuned into my own growth-possibilities? Do I have dreams which I am trying to turn into realities? If so, what am I doing to make them happen for me?

Am I open to new challenges, both personally and professionally? How do I respond to things that are unfamiliar? Am I open to new experiences, new places, new people? Or do I find myself doing the same things, in the same places, with the same people day after day?

Am I really living?

Am I really alive?

Effective communication: how to make it happen

Our communication has to do with our perceptions. When you and I are talking with one another, we are trading perceptions about the subject of our discussion. Our messages are really nothing other than statements of our perceptions of a certain reality: this film, that teacher, these people, and so on. All too often, however, we trade messages as though they were indisputable facts, as though we were saying the final word about whatever it is we are discussing.

We always have to remember that we are dealing not with cut-and-dried facts, but with perceptions. Not only do we have to recognize this ourselves; we have to make it clear to the other person as well. In other words, we always have to be aware of the fact that our messages are minority reports that reflect our individual and unique perceptions.

The question, then, is how to interject this awareness of the perceptual process into the communication situation in which we find ourselves. How can we shape our messages and responses so as to allow for the quirks of individual perception? There are several possibilities for us here. Here are some specific things that we can do to make our communication more effective:

The End: More effective communication
The Means: Description
     Quantification
     Personalization
     Clarification
     Amplification
     Flexibility and openness
     Active listening

Let's examine these "means" one at a time.

DESCRIPTION

Such statements as "he is conceited" or "she is a terrible professor" are meaningless. They say nothing at all about the persons to whom they refer; but they do say something about the speaker of the messages. They are evaluations, conclusions about a particular person. They are perceptions and nothing more. And yet, how often do we speak and hear such messages—presented not as perceptions but as dogmatic truth? Check out your own messages—listen for these evaluative statements—and you will undoubtedly hear yourself speaking them very often.

Well then, what to do? Try this and see if it helps: Instead of packaging your message in an evaluative judgment, make it a *description*. Instead of saying how you perceive this person, for example, tell what the person *did*. In other words, focus not so much on perceptions, but on observable behaviors. You may perceive a certain professor as "terrible" because she assigned eight novels as required reading for your Modern American Literature course, and you found that difficult to accomplish. But I may perceive it completely differently. I might enjoy reading those same eight novels and, consequently, may perceive the professor as "excellent."

Your report that she is a "terrible" professor says nothing at all about her. I know nothing about her or her expectations for her students, at least not on the basis of your message. Your message is useless. But when you rework that message so that it is a descriptive statement of behavior, then I have something with which to work. Let *me* make the judgment as to whether this or that requirement is excessive.

QUANTIFICATION

Quantification is closely related to description. When you tell me that this overcoat is "not expensive" or that the drive to Spanish Lake is "not far," you are not telling me anything. There is no information on the basis of which I can come to any conclusion in my own mind. How much in dollars and cents is "not expensive"—to whom and in what circumstances financially? You may have just received your Christmas bonus, and so a $190 coat is well within your reach. But that is not necessarily true for me. Instead of telling me that the coat is "not expensive," simply *quantify* your report and tell me that the coat costs $190. Let me decide whether or not that is "expensive"—after all, I am the one who will have to meet the payments.

The same is true with "not far." You may have a 3-day weekend coming up and, therefore, feel that you have all the time in the world. A 600-mile drive may not be "far" for you in that circumstance. But for me—in my particular circumstance, with my automobile's power-steering unit just about to go out—that same drive may well be out of the question. Instead of telling me that Spanish Lake is "not far," simply *quantify* your message and tell me exactly *how far* in miles. Let me decide whether or not that is "far" for me in my present situation.

This kind of quantification is so simple that it may seem obvious to you. But, here again, check yourself out. Take an inventory of the messages you send and hear how many times you fail to include such quantification. And then realize that those messages have absolutely no meaning for your listeners! They are your personal perceptions and nothing more.

PERSONALIZATION

We have been saying all along that our messages are minority reports. Any evaluative statement simply reflects my personal value judgment. Personalization is a means of giving voice to this personal dimension of the message. It is easy to include this in your message: Just preface your statement of perception by saying, "To me. . . ."; or, "It seems to me that. . . ."; or, "In my judgment. . . ." Any such phrase will serve the purpose.

This kind of personalization is also important in your capacity as a responder to the statement of another person. Here you simply preface your response with, "What I hear you saying is. . . ." This allows you to double-check the effectiveness of the transaction: You are announcing to the other person exactly what you "heard" him say—the meaning you attach to his message. Remember that because of the way in which perception works, what he "said" and what you "heard" are not necessarily the same. In order to find out how "together" you are in the communication, personalize your response. Then if you heard him incorrectly, he can restate his message.

CLARIFICATION

Clarification is a kind of summary-device to the end of more effective communication. Each of the other things we have recommended is designed to move us in the direction of increased clarity in our messages. We must always seek this clarity in the messages we send—and we must demand it in the messages we receive. *Say what you mean.* And if there is the slightest bit of doubt in your mind, *ask the other person what he means.* There is no room for chance-taking in communication. Too much is at stake, and the risks are great enough as it is. The more you leave to chance, the greater the possibility of ambiguity and misunderstanding.

AMPLIFICATION

Here we are recommending that you must be ready and able to expand on your message, including whatever particulars and specifics are requested or are necessary for understanding. If you are not able to supply this amplification, it may indicate that you are speaking with only half a notion about the subject of your message. If that is the case, then you become a kind of name-dropper, in that you are sending a message about something with which you may be only vaguely familiar.

We are not recommending that you burden your messages unnecessarily, loading them down with irrelevant facts and cumbersome data. This can make you a very tiresome communicator. We all have had the uncomfortable experience of listening to someone drone on and on about a film, for example, filling his messages with each and every detail—so much so that he comes across as a terrible bore (and a boor, as well!).

We are recommending that you be familiar enough with your subject to amplify your message if and when it is necessary to communicate more effectively your ideas. As a general rule of thumb, this is a good one: **If you do not know what you are talking about, you should be listening to find out.**

FLEXIBILITY AND OPENNESS

We have already talked about the life-world, the psychic space each one of us inhabits. If the contents of that life-world (your values, attitudes, beliefs, and so on) are rigidly defined— if they are finished once and for all—then you are definitely handicapped as a communicator. You are diminished in your ability to relate to other people because you will have closed yourself off to them, just as you will have closed yourself off to all sorts of experiences.

One social psychologist, Milton Rokeach, has distinguished between the person with an *open mind* and the person with a *closed mind*. According to Rokeach, each one of us has a "belief system" and a "disbelief system." Inside your belief system reside all those things with which you agree or in which you believe. And, of course, inside your disbelief system reside all those things with which you disagree or in which you do not believe. If you are a Roman Catholic, for example, the teachings and doctrines of the Church are a part of your belief system. The dogma of other denominations, in turn, is a part of your disbelief system. Input for these belief and disbelief systems comes from a number of sources: parental training, social experiences, educational background, and so on.

The effective communicator is in touch with his belief and disbelief systems. He knows what he believes and what he disbelieves, but he has an open mind, in that he is open to further information about the issues that make up his disbelief system. In other words, he is not completely rigid in his beliefs; the boundaries of his belief and disbelief systems are penetrable. Figure 7 diagrams the belief and disbelief systems.

Rokeach breaks down any communication event into two parts: the speaker and his message. As a listener, you may either accept or reject the speaker; and you may either accept or reject his message. These, then, are your possible responses in a given communication situation:

1. You may accept the speaker and accept his message.
2. You may accept the speaker but reject his message.

Figure 7 (Above) In this interaction, each person is a "closed system." The attitudinal boundaries are impenetrable, and, therefore, the channel of communication is blocked forever. Neither person can really hear the other. (Below) The attitudinal boundaries here are at least penetrable, and, therefore, the channel of communication is open. There will not necessarily be agreement; but at least there is communication.

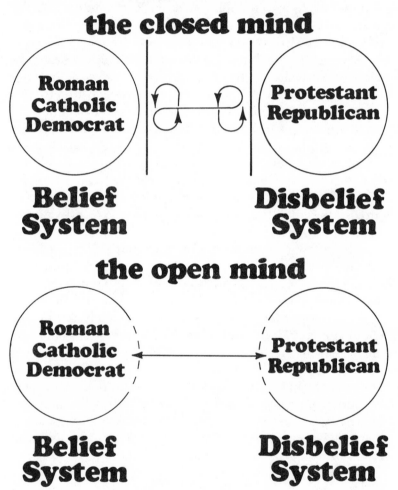

the closed mind

Roman Catholic Democrat

Protestant Republican

Belief System

Disbelief System

the open mind

Roman Catholic Democrat

Protestant Republican

Belief System

Disbelief System

3. You may reject the speaker and reject his message.

4. You may reject the speaker but accept his message.

If your mind is closed, options 1 and 3 are your only possibilities. Your belief and disbelief systems are so rigidly defined that you must either accept or reject both the speaker and his message. Consider, for example, the person who adamantly insists that he could *never* vote for a Republican (or Democrat), irrespective of his specific political program. Or the person who—election after election—votes not for the man, but for the party with which he is aligned. The closed-minded person reduces everything to an "either-or" proposition: Things are either black or white; everyone is either a "good guy" or a "bad guy."

But if your mind is open, all four options are possible for you. You are able to distinguish between the speaker and his message. You can transcend labels that may not be a part of your belief system. The open-minded person, for example, recognizes that not all Democrats are inherently good and all Republicans inherently bad (or vice versa) just because he aligns himself in principle with the general platform/position of a given political party.

Expanding the boundaries of your belief system is crucial to effective communication. Check yourself out in this regard. See and hear yourself in situations where you "tune out" a message simply because of its source. Then imagine what you are missing. We are not recommending that you indiscriminately believe everything you hear. But we are recommending that you at least *hear* everything that is said, that you *listen* to the messages you hear and consider them carefully. Only then will you be able to make reasonable and sound decisions. Only then will you be effective in your encounters with other people.

LISTENING

One of the most important factors in effective communication is listening. You cannot speak any better than you listen, precisely because your response to any message is always just that—a response. And if you have not been listening to the message (not just hearing it with your ears alone, but really listening with all your senses tuned into the speaker), then how can you articulate a meaningful response? The answer, of course, is that you cannot.

Too many of us, I am afraid, take listening for granted. Or worse, we consider listening an inconvenience, something that gets in the way of our own message-sending. Many of us seem to look on listening as an interruption of our own monologues. Check yourself out in this regard. See yourself in situations where your listening time may have been spent not listening at all, but, rather, putting together in your mind the next message you planned to send. The curious thing is that your listening—and the way in which you listen—is a message in its own right. Your partner in the communication will pick up on how well you are listening to him. He will perceive you as either *really* listening, or as just hearing the words but missing their real meaning.

The Components of Listening

Reception of Sound

Listening is a complex process, involving many different elements. First of all, of course, we hear sounds. Stimuli from all around us bombard our auditory nerves; these nerves pick up on the sound-wave stimuli and send them on to the brain. The precise physiology of the process is much more

44

complicated than that, of course. But, for our purposes, just be aware that the ears' reception of sound is only the very beginning of the listening process.

Recognition

The second step in the process is the recognition of sound. This, too, is a complicated process. In essence, it works like this: Even as we hear the sound, we are making *associations* in our minds. We recognize sounds not simply as noises, but as *realities*. For example, we hear the roar of the crowd at the Super Bowl and recognize it for what it is. We do not simply hear noise crashing against our eardrums; we hear people cheering their heroes and booing the bad guys.

Likewise do we recognize the scream of the child—not *any* scream of *any* child, but *this* scream of *our* child. We recognize the place of the scream and may hurry up the stairs to the baby's bedroom. All of this happens very quickly, of course, and much of it is prereflective. You do not hear the scream and then sit down to think it through. The hearing and the recognition occur simultaneously.

Meaning Giving

The third step in the process is the giving of meaning to the sound you have heard and recognized. This step builds on the other two, of course, and therefore is closely related to them. But the assignment of a certain meaning to the sound is a more discriminate event. For example, you hear a noise and recognize it as your child's scream coming from the up-stairs bedroom. You may or may not panic, depending on the meaning you assign to the scream. In addition to brute noise, you also hear innuendos of inflection, pitch and volume—all of which tell you whether the scream "means" that the child is in trouble or is simply squealing in the delight of fanciful play. In the one instance, you hurry up the stairs; in the other, you smile and continue reading your magazine.

In other words, there are cues beyond the noise or sound itself. And these cues go a long way toward your understanding of what you hear. We refer to these cues as *metacommunication* (from the Greek, *meta*, meaning *beyond*). Metacommunication can be defined as a "nonverbal message about a message." In the instance just cited, vocal metacommunication serves as a major determining factor in our understanding of the meaning of the scream. There are many other types of metacommunication: clothing, a gesture, a look, the physical distance you maintain between you and the person with whom you are speaking. All of these things serve to supplement spoken messages.

More Effective Listening Behavior

We all need to be heard; we all have the need to express ourselves. But we also need to listen. Otherwise communication becomes a kind of talking to oneself. Effective listening is not something that comes naturally to us. It is something we do; it is an activity. Effective listening is something each of us has to work on if we are serious about becoming more effective communicators. But how do we go about making our listening more effective? Here are some suggestions:

Listen Not for Words Alone but for Meanings

We have to pay close attention to the totality of the messages we hear. The effective listener is sensitive not only to the words, but to all the metacommunicative cues he hears and sees. He does not ask, "What do these *words* say?" Instead he asks, "What is this *person* trying to say with these words?"

Do Not Interrupt

One of the biggest obstacles to effective communication is my tendency to shut you up too soon, to cut you off before you have had the chance to say what you mean to say. I must discipline myself so that I do not respond until you have completed your thoughts.

Suspend as Much as Possible Your Own Prejudgments

Like everyone else, the effective listener has his own attitudes and biases. But he does not let these get in the way of his listening. This is important: If you do not suspend your prejudgments, then a single word ("Communist" or "homosexual," for example) can trigger an immediate emotional response, with the result that the rest of the message—the totality of the message—escapes you.

Listen first and understand what is being said. Then and only then see how the message fits in with your own individual life-world. Obviously, you do not have to accept every message which you receive. Not at all! But how can you make that determination unless you listen with an open mind to the message?

Avoid Unconscious Projection

Let the other person *be*. I must be very careful to avoid projecting myself (and where I am, emotionally and intellectually) onto the other person. I must let him be his own self, and let him speak who and where he is at this particular moment.

When most of us listen, we are asking ourselves the question, "What do these words mean to *me*?" Well, that's the wrong question. We should be asking ourselves, "What do these words mean to *him*?" The answer to this question will help us to get at the other person's meaning, at his intention.

Be Conscious of Your Own Metacommunication

Remember that even before you verbalize a response, you are sending nonverbal messages. Be aware of what counter-messages your metacommunication is sending the speaker. Even as you are listening, your metacommunication may be causing the speaker to become reluctant to continue as he wishes; your metacommunication may cause him to become defensive and make him choose his words so carefully that he may not say what wants (or needs) to say. A disapproving look, for example, may cause the speaker to back away from what he really wanted to say.

AWARENESS 3

The good therapist knows full-well that active, empathic listening is at the heart of the healing process. When I listen to you, I am giving you a freedom of speech. I am saying, in effect, "Go ahead, it's OK to feel that way and to report it to me." And my freeing you from your fear and hesitancy is a great gift to you.

Here is how good listening can help you to heal yourself: When I am listening to you, you are also listening to yourself. You are hearing yourself, maybe for the first time. And the more you hear yourself as you really are, the more clear your situation becomes in your mind. After awhile you are in a position to say, "Ah, that's what it's all about. And now this is what I must do. . . ."

It sounds easy. And it is, once we start to listen—to ourselves and to one another—in an open and accepting way.

THE TRANSITION

Putting communication to work

To this point we have talked about specific ways of making ourselves more effective communicators. Now we are going to talk about becoming more in touch with ourselves as persons, more genuine and authentic in speaking about who we are. We play out our lives—for better or worse—in relationships. And those relationships all hinge on communication. **The more authentic our communication, the more satisfying our relationships will be.**

My experience listening to people of all ages and backgrounds—students, parents, husbands, wives, lovers— tells me that there is widespread disaffection and estrangement among us. The most fundamental estrangement, and the most crippling, is *self-alienation*: that condition in which we are out of touch with our feelings, needs, and desires. The result of such self-alienation is a diminished person who is no longer in charge of his behaviors and who, consequently, is unable to establish meaningful relationships with others. The self-alienated person is a stranger to himself.

A related estrangement is *other-alienation*: that condition in which we are out of touch with the feelings, needs, and desires of those people around us. The result of such other-alienation is a person whose relationships are lacking in intimacy and significance. The other-alienated person remains forever a stranger to other people.

This is what we are about as we begin to put effective communication to work: *Getting ourselves together and translating that togetherness into better relationships.*

AUTHENTIC
COMMUNICATION

Getting
it all
together

Authentic communication is effective communication taken one step further. It is a communication experience that takes place between two or more "whole" persons, coming together in an honest, open, truly human kind of encounter. A "whole" person is one who knows who he or she is in relation to other people and who seeks out other people in an attempt to establish significant, meaningful relationships that will be growth-producing for everyone concerned.

Not everyone is capable of entering into authentic communication, at least not right away; getting yourself ready for this very special kind of communication is a growth-process in itself. It requires a keen critical awareness of yourself in relation to those around you. Developing that awareness— and learning how to act upon it—is what this section is all about.

Understanding
the self

The literature of contemporary "pop" psychology is filled with book after book dealing with "better" ways to understand and appreciate who you are as an individual. Some of these books provide metaphors of the self—images of what the self is like; others provide models for understanding the self and individual behavior. In this section, we will deal with some commonplace metaphors and models. Our aim is to come to an increased awareness of who we are as persons. Our thesis is this: **You cannot understand yourself in relationships unless you first understand yourself as an individual.**

METAPHORS OF THE SELF

The Mirror Self

This metaphor suggests that a person comes to know himself as a self insofar as he interacts with other people and, in the process of that interaction, receives feedback from others.

The metaphor is a useful one because it recognizes the tremendous impact other people have on you as an individual. Think back, for example, to what it was like for you when you first began school. You may have been 5 or 6 or 7 years old, still very much a beginner in terms of the development of an awareness of your own self. You had absolutely no idea as to who you were as a student, because you had never *been* a student before. Well then, how did your awareness of "you as student" develop? It developed as a result of the feedback you received from your teachers and your fellow-students, of course. You were continually evaluated in terms of your in-school performance. And the end-result of those evaluations was a picture of yourself—in your own mind—as a student.

The metaphor of the *mirror self* focuses on the importance of communication on your personal growth and development. You can also use this metaphor to understand the impact you have on other persons. For example, think about the feedback you provide for your parents, brothers and sisters, children, and friends. Is that feedback positive and constructive or is it negative and destructive? (Remember, now, that this feedback goes a long way toward determining their pictures of themselves.)

We are talking here about the effect of so-called labeling behavior, an effect called *self-fulfilling prophecy*. This simply means that if you label yourself a failure as a student, for example, you will perform whatever behaviors are necessary to bring about an actual failure in your studies. Similarly, if your parents, teachers, and the courts label you as incorrigible, you will perform behaviors that will "prove"—to yourself and to them—that, in fact, you are incorrigible. Self-fulfilling prophecy is simply the actualizing in behavior of whatever labels are assigned to you (either by others or by yourself). Figure 9 shows how it works.

Assumptions
  Inferences
    Behavior

Figure 9

Assumptions

Assumptions refer to the beliefs you maintain about yourself. The metaphor of the *mirror self* suggests that much of the input for these assumptions comes from without: parents, teachers, ministers, friends—all of these people (and many more) tell you who you are. But these assumptions also come from within, inasmuch as it is your responsibility to mediate the feedback you get from other people: You accept some of that feedback as valid, but reject some as invalid.

Inferences

Inferences refer to the conclusions which a person arrives at about himself. These conclusions are directly related to his assumptions about himself. If a man assumes, for example, that he is of little worth as an individual, he will conclude that he need not strive to make something of himself; he figures that it is just not worth the effort. And—in terms of his behavior—he will abdicate responsibility for his actions. If, on the other hand, this same man assumes that he is worth something as an individual, he will conclude that he can indeed make something of himself. And—in terms of his behavior—he will set about actualizing his potential to the fullest.

Behavior

Behavior refers to the things we do. Some of the things we do are pretty obvious: Shoving someone out of our way, for example, is a blatant behavior. But some of the things we do are not so obvious: An angry look or a mean word is behavior, too. It is important that we understand that everything we do—verbal or nonverbal—is a behavior.

The Onion Self

This metaphor finds its inspiration in Ibsen's poetic drama, *Peer Gynt*. Ibsen shows a man who is put together much like an onion—layer upon layer of "skin," with no core, no center, no substance. The metaphor is a good one: When you peel an onion, you can unravel the skin until there is nothing left.

The metaphor of the *onion self* is suggestive of the kind of person who is all external pretense and show. This person is a kind of social chameleon: He changes himself over and over again as a means of manipulating the people around him. He "is" whatever he needs to be at a given moment in order to attain what he wants.

The Chooser Self

The metaphor of the *chooser self* is extremely rich in insight. It suggests that—in spite of pressure and direction from without—man retains control of and responsibility for

The question
of communion:
a beginning

Communion means a "being-with." It refers to the undeniable human reality that ours is a shared existence. From the moment of your first conscious awareness, there are other people present. Growing up, then, becomes largely a matter of learning to satisfy your own personal needs without trampling on the needs of others. The most basic question we must ask in regard to authentic communication is this: What is the nature of my "being-with" others? This question forces us to become more aware of the kind of communion we establish with other persons, most especially our intimates.

Phatic Communication

If you pay close attention to your everyday messages, you will undoubtedly discover that many of them are rather mundane and simplistic. For example, on your way to the bus stop one morning, you run into someone whom you recognize from the neighborhood. She says, "Hi," and you respond, "How're you doing?" But that is the extent of the interaction. Each of you continues on your respective way. You have engaged in *phatic communication*.

Phatic communications are those trite, uninspired messages that are normally used to communicate simple recognition, rather than a specific meaning. Common pleasantries make up phatic communication. In the instance just cited, for example, by asking "How're you doing?," you are neither seeking nor expecting the other person to stop and tell you how she is. She realizes this, of course, and so she does not stop to tell you in detail how she is.

Admittedly, phatic communication is not very significant. It really does not say anything. And yet phatic communication serves an important social function. After all, it is a friendly recognition of the fact that the other person is there and that you acknowledge her. It serves to open—or to keep open—the channels of communication.

Phatic Communion

Given its limitations, phatic communication serves a definite social function. *Phatic communion* is something else. Communion is a broader concept than communication. As already noted, *communion* refers to the state of your coexistence with other people. Individual communications—when put together—constitute communion (see Figure 8).

There are some persons who never get beyond the level

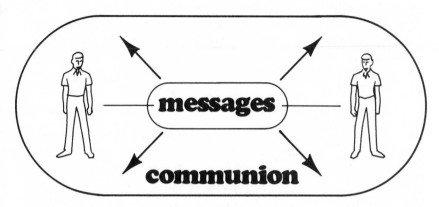

Figure 8

of phatic communication, not even with members of their own family. I have counseled countless men and women who may have been married for 15 or 20 or 30 years and yet who—in all that time—have never *really met* one another! They live together, but never really talk with one another; they never share their feelings and secret dreams and fears and innermost concerns. They may be sexually intimate, but they remain strangers to one another.

It is not only husbands and wives who sometimes live together while remaining strangers to one another. A man once came to see me about an unbearable situation at home. He complained that he had given his teenaged son all kinds of material things and could not understand why his boy remained cold and aloof toward him. This man felt bitter about what he saw as his son's lack of appreciation. After we talked for a little while, he began to see what had happened: He had given his son everything but what he needed most—a father with whom he could really talk and in whom he could really confide.

When you coexist in a relationship without ever getting beyond the level of exchanging phatic messages, then you find yourself in a state of phatic communion. Phatic communion is a very unsatisfying experience; in fact it is a pseudo-relationship, one that retards the growth of all involved.

Authentic Communion

Authentic communion is anything but phatic. It is a very special way of being with other people, especially intimates. Authentic communion requires a deep-rooted understanding of the self; an appreciation of your own uniqueness, as well as the uniqueness of others; a receptivity to the ideas and values of other people; and a commitment to enhancing the depth and intensity of your relationships. As we continue in our discussion, we will be pushing you in the direction of this authentic kind of communion.

AWARENESS 4

Communication really involves two different but related processes:

Sensibility and Responsibility

Let's do it like this:

Sense-ability   and   Response-ability

Sense-ability is the ability to sense what is really happening in any given situation, to be sensitive to your own feelings and needs and to the feelings and needs of those around you.

Response-ability is the ability to respond to your own feelings and needs, to respond to the feelings and needs of those around you.

---

his own destiny. The metaphor suggests that behavior is choice, that we—as individuals—choose the course of our own lives.

This is a very important awareness. Many persons—as soon as we raise the issue—will respond by asking if perhaps these choices we make are not often unconscious. That seems to me to be a rationalization. Perhaps many of the choices we make are unconscious, in the sense that we are not aware of them as we are making them. But the fact remains that we are making choices all the time. It is not helpful to talk about these choices as "conscious" or "unconscious," because that allows us to shirk responsibility for them, figuring that if they are unconscious, they cannot be helped.

It is much more helpful to force ourselves to recognize those choices we make and then to ask whether they are *productive* or *counterproductive* in terms of our own personal growth. We can expand that question to include the notion of the ecology of human relationships: Are these choices conducive to healthy interpersonal relationships or are they detrimental to those relationships?

Summing Up

We have outlined three metaphors of the self—three word-pictures to help us understand better what the self is like. None of these metaphors (by itself) is adequate to explain the complexity of the human person. Putting all three of them together, however, can be useful in helping you to understand who you are. By way of summary then:

The metaphor of the *mirror self* suggests the reality that there are a great many external influences on your concept of your own self. It reminds us that feedback from others, in large part, determines how we picture ourselves.

The metaphor of the *onion self* reminds us that, inevitably, we play a number of social roles. And it cautions us that we must be careful lest we lose ourselves in these roles. When we lose ourselves in the roles which we play, we become *self-alienated*, strangers to ourselves. We no longer know who we are in relation to other people. The self-alienated person is crippled in his ability to establish significant interpersonal relationships.

The metaphor of the *chooser self* alerts us to the fact that we must hold ourselves responsible for the behavioral choices we make even though others influence us. We cannot blame our shortcomings and failings on others. *We* are the masters of our *own* destinies.

ROLES AND ROLE-PLAYING

In order to fully understand your own self, it is necessary to understand the concepts of *roles* and *role-playing*. A role is simply a behavioral function in a given social system. Think for a minute and count the number of roles you play: a son or a daughter in your family; perhaps a brother or a sister, a husband or a wife, a father or mother; maybe an employee in the store where you work or a part-time student at the community college. These may be only some of the roles you play. There are probably many more.

When we talk about role-playing in my classes, students often respond in a negative way; they think we are talking about something phony and superficial. Such a negative response is unwarranted, however, if you understand what a role is. (The problem here might be a semantic one: The very phrase, *role-playing*, suggests something that is false.)

In actuality, role-playing is a neutral behavior—it is neither good nor bad. It is simply a social fact. *Playing a role* simply means that you perform a certain social function. It is not a question of whether or not you *will* play a social role—inevitably you play many of them. The question, rather, is *how* do you play your various roles? With what degree of effectiveness? And what do you derive from the roles which you play?

Psychologist Sidney Jourard points out that the "normal" person is able to play his various social roles with a considerable amount of effectiveness and efficiency. But Jourard recognizes that this "normal" person is not necessarily a "healthy" person. The healthy person plays his roles in a socially acceptable way. But, more importantly, he also derives personal satisfaction from the playing of those roles. This is a very important insight, a significant awareness: **Normal is *not* the same as healthy**.

I have a friend who is a highly successful businessman in a large eastern city. He is quite "normal" in his business role: He conducts his professional affairs in a very effective way, reaping high returns on his financial investments. But more and more he had begun to experience bouts of depression. The more he and I talked about what was happening to him, the more obvious it was that he was perfectly miserable in his role: He was putting little real effort into it and was deriving little or no personal satisfaction from what he was doing. He was playing his role in such a way that he was simply putting in his time and not getting any personal return on the investment of his energy.

Recently my friend and I have been exploring ways in which he might turn things around and play his businessman-role in a "healthy" way. He has come to realize that—at least in terms of his time—being a businessman is an important dimension of who he is at this point in his life, so he has determined to make of his businessman-role everything he can. He is putting more real effort into his role-performance and is beginning to experience a sense of satisfaction from doing a job well. The point is simple enough: For the *healthy* person, being a businessman (or student, or parent, or employee, or whatever) is not tedious, but challenging!

It is inevitable, then, that we perform certain roles in society. But we always have to remember that we are not the roles we play. We are simply persons *filling* those roles. And we have to learn to *fulfill* ourselves as persons in the process of playing our various roles. Some persons lose sight of this fact and become obsessed with the role itself; they lose themselves in the roles they play. **The authentic person does not lose sight of his own self in the myriad of social roles he plays. Rather, he uses these roles as springboards to his continued self-growth.**

DELAYED GRATIFICATION

Many people tend to put off achieving satisfaction and fulfillment until some vague future date. This delaying of gratification is one of the reasons for widespread feelings of frustration with the present situation and feelings of disenchantment with the self. I have counseled many students who have fallen into this trap. I remember one student especially who saw her college years as only preparatory for the beginning of her "real" life. She lived for graduation day when she would have—at long last—that diploma (as though the diploma itself were some kind of ticket to instant fame and fortune and happiness). This is a very unrealistic view—and a harmful one, as well. Such students live *in and for* the future, which means, of course, that they are not living at all *right now*. They are merely existing, or—even worse—enduring.

Many persons lock themselves into this delayed gratification as a kind of life-pattern. There is always that "something else" toward which they are aiming: after the diploma, that prestigious job; after the job, that promotion; after the promotion, that mortgage-free home in the suburbs; and on and on and on, until, one day, they realize that they have spent their entire lives chasing after a nonexistent pot of gold at the end of the rainbow.

I am not saying that you should not have aspirations or goals. I am not suggesting that you forego planning for the future. But I am saying that you have to live in the present, making the most of each and every day which is given to you. The healthy, together person is the one who plays out his various roles in such a way that he attains a sense of achievement and satisfaction in the process—right now!

MODELS OF THE SELF

In addition to the three metaphors described, there are also several models that can help us to understand the self. We will deal with two such models. The first is a model commonly used in workshops, seminars, and training sessions on interpersonal communication. I call this model a *Component Model of the Self*, because it focuses on the various component parts of who you are as a person.

The second model is *Transactional Analysis* (TA). TA is an extremely popular and productive model of the self, and its study is a worthwhile venture. Let's take a look at each of these models in turn.

A COMPONENT MODEL OF THE SELF

We are complex beings, so much so, that understanding ourselves requires a consideration of the various component parts that make up the self. The first component is a physical one: You are a certain height and a certain weight; your hair is a certain color and so are your eyes. These physical characteristics are a part of you. We can refer to the composite of these physical characteristics as the *Empirical Self* (see Figure 10). When I see you in a crowd, recognize you and greet you with a wave of the hand, I am acknowledging your Empirical Self.

the empirical self: 5'9" 170 lbs. brown hair, brown eyes,... etc.

Figure 10

There is much more to you as a person than the Empirical Self. And so we have to add a second component to the model—what we call the *Pictured Self*. This Pictured Self is the psychological estimation you have of yourself; the image of "you" that you carry around in your head. For example, you may picture yourself as attractive or unattractive, coordinated or uncoordinated, intelligent or slow, and so on. What you believe about yourself is what the Pictured Self is all about (see Figure 11).

The plot thickens. But we are not done yet. There is still another component to be considered—one we call the *Pro-*

the pictured self: attractive, coordinated, intelligent,...etc.

the empirical self: 5'9" 170 lbs. brown hair, brown eyes,...etc.

Figure 11

jected Self. Inside the Projected Self reside your ambitions, hopes, dreams, and desires, everything you *want* to be or to become. The Projected Self is future-oriented (see Figure 12).

Things to Do

1. Take a good look at your own Empirical Self. Get in touch with what you look like. See yourself as others see you when they run into you on the street. Use a full-length mirror for this exercise. Let go of some of your inhibitions and really study yourself. Play around with different facial expressions and different bodily postures and movements:

Get Angry—really angry, perhaps at the thought of someone insulting you. And see what you look like when you feel this way. Look at what you do with your face. And with

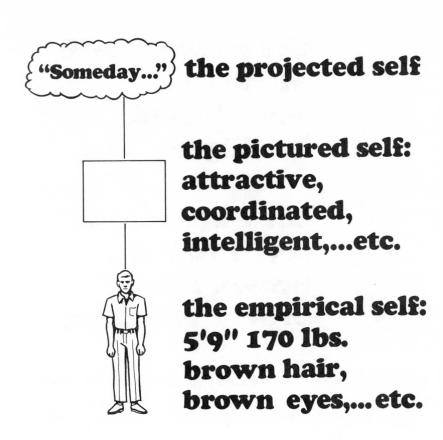

"Someday..." the projected self

the pictured self: attractive, coordinated, intelligent,...etc.

the empirical self: 5'9" 170 lbs. brown hair, brown eyes,...etc.

Figure 12

your body. This is what people see when they encounter an angry you.

Be Happy—really feel it by focusing mentally on something which pleases you. Look at what you do with your face. And with your body. This is what people see when they encounter a happy you.

Feel Down—it's OK! Really feel it by focusing mentally on something which makes you sad. Look at what you do with your face. And with your body. (Notice that you seem shorter now than you did a few minutes ago. This is because your shoulders are probably stooped in a wary, defensive posture. When you are feeling something with your emotions, your body follows suit and mirrors that feeling.)

2. Take an inventory of your Pictured Self. Here you simply need a pad and pencil, some concentration, a little introspection, and a lot of honesty with yourself. Let go of all your censors and let it flow—from your mind onto the paper—as best you can: How do you see yourself ? How do you feel about yourself ? Do you like yourself ? Do you respect yourself ? And, if so, how do you show it? These are really very important questions, inasmuch as a feeling of high self-esteem is central to all productive behavior.

3. Now open up your Projected Self and see what it is all about. Write it down; get it on paper. Maybe make a kind of calendar for yourself and then fill in the details: Where are you now, personally and professionally? Where do you want to be? In a year? In 5 years? What do you envision for your future? What are you doing right now to make that vision happen for you? What about your dreams and ambitions?

These are not idle exercises. Getting in touch with your various component selves is absolutely essential if you are going to understand who you are in relation to other people. Take another look at the finished model and then consider these things:

1. What kind of effect does your Empirical Self have on your Pictured Self ? Do you have certain physical characteristics that cause you to be especially self-conscious in this regard? Are you perhaps being harder on yourself than you have to be?

2. What about your Pictured Self ? How does your self-estimation affect your behavior? Again, is there a chance that you are being too hard on yourself, not giving yourself

enough credit for your unique abilities? If so, how can you turn this around? How can you rework your self-image so that it will move your behavior in a more positive and constructive direction? Study the dynamics of behavior shown in Figure 13. There is no doubt but that there is a direct correlation between the way in which you adjudge yourself and the way in which you behave.

Assumptions ⌐
Inferences ⌐
Behavior

Figure 13

3. What about your Projected Self? How realistic are your idealizations in light of your Empirical Self? For example, if you dream of being the starting center on the college's basketball team, but are only 5'8", then you are in for a big letdown—but only if you leave yourself open for that disappointment! Take stock of yourself and do not let your weaknesses frustrate you. Do not waste energy needlessly chasing ambitions which—for one reason or another—may simply be closed to you. Play to your strengths. Set goals for yourself. Make sure that they are attainable with effort. And then go after them with everything you have and all the energy you can muster. Your life will work *for* you if you work *at* it.

TRANSACTIONAL ANALYSIS

TA provides a very helpful model of the self in relation to others. TA focuses, first of all, on the way in which the individual is put together (structural analysis), and then on the ways in which people interact with one another (transactional analysis). The model of TA was first articulated by Eric Berne, a California psychiatrist, in his book, *Games People Play*.[1]

TA provides a model of the self to answer these questions:

1. *How do I behave?* The answer to this question enhances my awareness of my interpersonal behavior.
2. *Why do I behave this way?* The answer to this question increases my sensitivity to the forces and pressures—internal and external—that prompt my behavior.
3. *How did I get to this behavior?* The answer to this question helps me to understand the way in which I have developed and evolved into the person I am right now.
4. *Who am I?* This is the most fundamental of all questions, the answer to which is the key to understanding the self in communication with others.

TA finds its inspiration in the research work of a neurosurgeon, Wilder Penfield. Penfield discovered that by attaching electrodes to various parts of the brain and then stimulating those areas, he was able to have a patient recall feelings and experiences long-since forgotten at the level of conscious awareness. His research suggests that everything that happens to us is stored inside the brain, as though the brain were a kind of videotape recorder.

Eric Berne discerned the significance of Penfield's research and used it as the springboard for his notion of the *ego state*. Berne defines the ego state as a "consistent pattern of feeling and experience directly related to a corresponding consistent pattern of behavior." Figure 14 shows how it works.

[1]Eric Berne, *Games People Play* (New York: Grove Press, 1964).

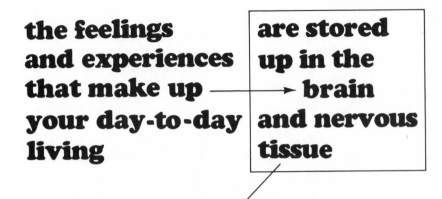

the feelings and experiences that make up your day-to-day living → **are stored up in the brain and nervous tissue**

and then show themselves in your behavior

Figure 14

In order to understand our behaviors, then, we have to take an inventory of our feelings and experiences and then listen to the messages these have recorded in our brain. These messages "speak" themselves in our behaviors.

Your Ego States

There are three ego states inside every person: the PARENT, the ADULT, and the CHILD. The popular expression, "Where are you coming from?," can be applied directly to these ego states. In terms of your behaviors, you "come from" either your PARENT, your ADULT, or your CHILD.

Your PARENT contains the messages you have picked up from the outside—from your mother and father, older brothers and sisters, teachers, ministers, and other authority figures. Your PARENT can be judgmental, stern, and threatening; but it can also be tender, compassionate, and loving. When you behave as you saw your parents and other authority figures behave—when you are influenced by what these persons taught you—you are behaving from your PARENT ego state.

Some of your parental messages are very helpful. But others can be limiting and confining, in that they may no longer be applicable to you now that you have grown and matured. The following are some messages commonly found in the PARENT ego state:

"Look both ways before crossing the street."

"Don't trust strangers."

"Help your little brother."

"Save your money."

"If you want anything in this life, you have to work for it."

"Study hard and make something of yourself."

The ADULT in you has nothing to do with your age. When you are coming from your ADULT, you are functioning as a fully thinking, intelligent person. Your ADULT confronts a situation in a forthright way and sets about working it through in the best way possible. The ADULT figures the various options at its disposal and chooses the best one in a dispassionate manner. When you are coming on from your ADULT in a consistent way, you never have to worry about your checkbook being out of balance—the ADULT takes care of that kind of thing very easily.

The CHILD in you contains all the emotions and feelings you experienced during your childhood. Your CHILD is curious, playful, energetic, creative, and spontaneous. But your CHILD is also selfish, whining, and manipulative.

There are three different dimensions to your CHILD:

1. The NATURAL CHILD is impulsive, willful, and fun-loving. The NATURAL CHILD loves a picnic, and may cry when rain spoils the good time. The NATURAL CHILD is fully a child and—like any child—a wonder to behold.

2. The LITTLE PROFESSOR busies himself with figuring things out. The LITTLE PROFESSOR knows how far he can go with people before they lose their tempers; and he will go *just far enough* to get what he wants. The LITTLE PROFESSOR is an emerging adult in that he is in the process of developing a social sense.

3. The ADAPTED CHILD is the end-product of parental training and example. No longer completely unrestrained and uninhibited, the ADAPTED CHILD learns to fit in with what his parents have told him about himself and his place in the world. Parental "DOS," "DON'TS," "SHOULDS," and "OUGHTS" weigh heavily on the ADAPTED CHILD.

Your responses to various experiences can be understood in light of Transactional Analysis. Consider, for example, a commonplace situation such as shopping around for a new automobile. Imagine that you visit one showroom and the salesman proudly (and somewhat eagerly) points out his most expensive model, a shiny sports car.

How do you respond to his sales pitch? If you come on from your PARENT, you may respond like this: "I'd never consider having a sports car. They're unsafe. And besides, I think that middle-aged people look foolish driving them, like they're trying to prove how young they are."

If you come on from your ADULT, you may respond like this: "It is beautiful, but I'm afraid that the payments would be too much for my budget. And the upkeep! What with the price of gasoline and all, I'm afraid that it just wouldn't be practical for me."

If you come on from your CHILD, you may respond like this: "What a car! I'll take it." (Most sales pitches, incidentally, seem to be aimed at the CHILD in us, precisely because of this tendency to be impulsive when responding from this ego state.)

Or imagine that you are working in an office and your supervisor comes to you with a rush typing job 30 minutes before quitting time.

How do you respond to the request? If you come on from your PARENT, you may respond like this: "This place is the most disorganized office I've ever seen. The work piles up till the last minute; then—all of a sudden—it's 'Rush, rush, rush.' I'd make a much more efficient supervisor than Mrs. Lawler."

If you come on from your ADULT, you may respond like this: "This must be an important report. And Mrs. Lawler needs it by five o'clock, so I'd better get going on it."

If you come on from your CHILD, you may respond like this: "No matter how hard I work, there's no pleasing that old battle-axe. Why does she always pick on me like this??!"

In the instances just cited, it is more appropriate for you to be coming on from your ADULT than from your PARENT or CHILD. In other instances, however, this may not be the case. If you are playing with your 4-year-old niece, for example, it is appropriate for you to come on from your CHILD so that you can have fun right along with her. Or if a friend of yours is grieving because of the death of his wife, it is appropriate for you to come on from your PARENT so that you can be with him in a supportive and comforting way.

The trick is in developing what we call an INTEGRATED ADULT. The person with this INTEGRATED ADULT is able to respond to any situation in an appropriate and productive way. This person is in touch with helpful messages in his PARENT and also with the more positive aspects of his CHILD. The person with an INTEGRATED ADULT is a "together" kind of person, in the sense that he retains the sensitivity, concern, and compassion of the PARENT; the problem-solving ability of the ADULT; and the energetic spontaneity and creativity of the CHILD.

The Language of TA

People who work with TA use a very special kind of language to describe the workings of the self in relation to others. The language of TA is simple enough, with vivid metaphors and images drawn from everyday experience— and that is the beauty and utility of it. There is no technical jargon, no confusing terminology to scare away the layman. Let us look at some of this language and see how it helps us to come to an understanding of the self.

Life Positions

A life position is the general, deep-seated attitude a person maintains about himself. There are four different life positions:

1. *I'm OK-You're OK*—This is the life position maintained by a person who is on the road toward growth and emotional maturity. The person who assumes this attitude recognizes his own worth and also acknowledges the worth of other people. This is where we want to be. The "together" person is honestly able to say: "I'm OK and you're OK. Neither of us is perfect, but we're both OK. I will not threaten you; nor will I be afraid to approach you, because I recognize that we can learn from and share with one another."

2. *I'm OK-You're not OK*—This is sometimes referred to as the *projective position*, in that the person with this attitude

projects all of his shortcomings, failings, and inadequacies onto others. This person often hears himself saying: "If only it weren't for . . . ," with the result, of course, that his life becomes a very desperate existence.

3. *I'm not OK-You're OK*—This is sometimes referred to as the *introjective position*, since the person becomes very down on himself. The person who maintains this attitude feels hopelessly inadequate in comparison with others. He feels unable to cope and, in fact, often becomes actually immobilized. This person tends to become depressed and—as a response to the depression—withdraws from interpersonal contact.

4. *I'm not OK-You're not OK*—This is referred to as the *futility position* because, for the person who assumes this attitude, life becomes nothing short of a futile and senseless endeavor. Life simply is not worth living for this person; neither he nor anyone else makes any sense or has any purpose or direction. For obvious reasons, this person is dangerous to himself and to others. He has nothing to lose, he figures, because—in his own mind—there is nothing there in the first place.

Life Scripts

Each person plays out his or her life according to a certain script. This script is a kind of gameplan for living, in that it provides cues and directions for individual behavior. This script can be thought of as similar to any script for any dramatic production: It includes a setting, a cast of characters, dialogue, and a sequence of events.

The content of your life script is determined, in part, by your life position, by parental messages, and by your experiences. Many of us get locked into an unproductive life script unwittingly. But then—for some reason—we seem bent on playing it out, even though we may be aware of its destructive nature. This happens too often, but it certainly is not inevitable. The trick is to be able to proofread your own life script and to determine whether or not it is a useful and productive one. If your judgment is that your life script is not productive, then set about rewriting it. Break out of any dead-end behavioral patterns in which you may find yourself trapped. Rework your script, eliminating what you deem detrimental to your continued self-growth.

Strokes

There is ample research evidence to suggest that we all need attention and recognition from other people. The "maternal deprivation syndrome," for example, is the designation we use for a very real phenomenon: If a child is ignored—denied fondling, nursing, and other tactile stimulation—he or she will become sick. If this lack of touching is severe enough and prolonged, the child may die. Something in the human being requires this tender, loving care and attention.

In TA, this touching is called *stroking*. When another person recognizes or acknowledges you, he is giving you a stroke. These strokes can be positive or negative, and, obviously, the positive stroke is the more desirable of the two. But it seems to me that—for most of us—even a negative stroke is better than no stroke at all. (This may help to explain the teenager who engages in delinquent behavior, because then at least his parents will have to get *somewhat* involved with him.)

Positive strokes are helping and supportive. They range from the minimal "hello" to "I need you" or "I love you." Negative strokes imply what is called a *discount* of the other person, with the result that there is an emotional hurt.

Stamps

The feelings that accompany stroking behavior are called *stamps*. The good, warm feelings that go along with a positive stroke are called *gold stamps*; the not-so-good, not-so-warm feelings that go along with a negative stroke are called *brown stamps*. We can also talk about *anger stamps, envy stamps*, and so on. The image is simple enough: When someone does something which makes you feel good, you have collected a gold stamp.

Gold stamps really do not present much of a problem (other than the fact that—for some of us—they may be in short supply). But brown stamps can be very troublesome. Many of us become "stamp collectors," in the sense that we save up all of our bad feelings, letting them build and fester inside until we cannot take it any longer—then we "cash in" the stamps in a fight or a confrontation. The curious thing, of course, is that the fight inevitably is counterproductive. And generally it comes about as the result of the most incidental and trivial of happenings. The emotional explosion does not make sense because it is out of context and after the fact.

We will be returning to the question of the repression of feelings and the devastating effect which this can have on a relationship. For the moment, just be aware of the fact that we simply must get in touch with our feelings and be able to speak them—to ourselves and to others—in an open, honest, and forthright way.

Things to Do

It is important that you get in touch with each of your ego states: with the PARENT, CHILD, and ADULT inside you. By doing this, you can come to a greater appreciation of the complexity of your self and a greater awareness of just exactly who you are and why you behave as you do. All that is required here is a little imagination and considerable patience. It requires effort, but the results are well worth that effort.

Getting in Touch with Your PARENT

Again, let's look at our model of the dynamic of human behavior (see Figure 15). Many of the assumptions you maintain about yourself are derived from parental messages. It is

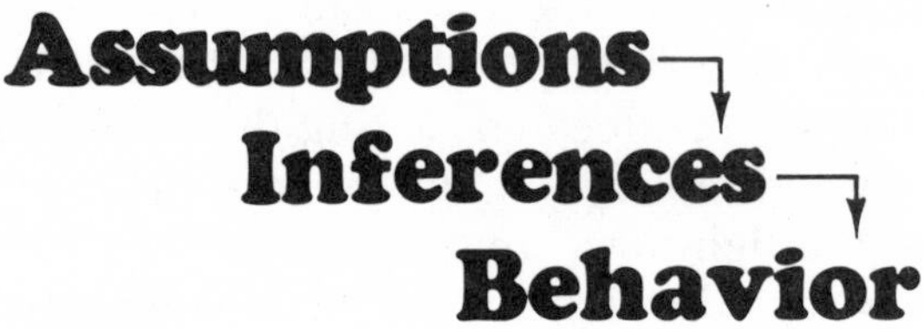

Assumptions￢
     Inferences￢
          Behavior

Figure 15

imperative, then, that you get in touch with these messages, that you listen to them carefully and with a critical/aware ear. You can do it like this:

Imagine just as vividly as you can all the authority figures who influenced you when you were a child. See them in your mind's eye, just as clearly as you can. To assist your imagination here, climb up into the attic and dust off that old photograph album. Go through it, from the beginning, and see all the people who were there when you were small: your mother and father, of course; maybe your grandmother and grandfather or an older brother or sister who had charge over you; a minister or a teacher, perhaps, who influenced you in one way or another. All these persons—and maybe more—helped to shape your PARENT ego state. And all of them are living in your PARENT right now. See all of them in your mind. Really see them.

Now listen to them. Listen to the messages they gave (and continue to give) you. Hear them speaking to you. Hear what they are telling you about:

Money

Success

Fun

Religion

Sexuality

You

Perhaps the last one *(You)* is the most important of them all. What did these parent-figures tell you about you. And how does this affect your self-estimation right now?

Now it is a matter of evaluating these parental messages. Undoubtedly many of them are still very valuable; maybe even life-saving. For example, "Look both ways before crossing the street" is one parental message you should never erase.

But perhaps some of these parental tapes are outdated and no longer useful to you. More than that, some of them could actually be harmful. For example, "Never trust strangers." Is that old tape hindering you—right now—from seeking out new people and taking some of the risks that are necessary in the development of intimate relationships? The tape may have been useful to you when you were 5 or 6 or 7 years old; it is outdated now, however, and it should be erased.

And what about your perceptions of the world and other people? Is there an old parental tape running in your head which says that getting by in this world is a matter of "survival of the fittest"? If so, does this tape determine your approach to others? Does it prevent you from trusting them and confiding in them, for fear that they might betray you?

I am not recommending here that you erase all your parental tapes. As has already been noted, many of them may well be helpful to you. But in order to make that determination, you first have to hear them with a critical ear. Save the tapes that are helpful. But erase the ones that are outdated and no longer valid given your present situation.

Getting in Touch with Your CHILD

Go back to the photograph album. This time, pick out those pictures of you when you were 5 or 6 or 7 years old. What did you look like? See yourself as you were then. Maybe focus on a picture when you were wearing your favorite outfit, the one that brings back all kinds of memories. Really see yourself—as you were—as a child.

Now tune into what it felt like to be a child. How did it feel, for example, to be in a world in which very nearly everybody was taller than you? How did you handle that feeling? Did you try to assert yourself and become your own person? Or did you use your lack of physical stature as a ploy to manipulate others and to get what you wanted?

Listen to the hurts, the fears, the joys of your childhood. Recall a time—a real event—when you were happy: What did that feel like? How did you respond in that situation? Now recall a time when you were sad: What did that feel like? And how did you behave then?

Now get in touch with the CHILD in you right now. See yourself having fun: at a party or on a picnic or at the beach. How do you behave? How do you have fun? Is it a relaxed, uninhibited, spontaneous experience? Or do you check yourself? If so, why do you feel the need to censor and restrain yourself?

What about the pains and disappointments you experience right now? How do you handle these? What does it feel like when you are hurting? How do you respond to the hurt?

To whom do you turn in these moments of emotional pain? Is the hurt honestly expressed? Or do you sometimes use it in a minipulative way to win sympathy or special considerations?

Getting in Touch with—
and Integrating—Your ADULT

For the moment, block out your PARENT as best you can. Turn off the tape recorder in your head, so that the messages do not come through.

For the moment, block out your CHILD as best you can. Forget your hurts and fears and anxieties and disappointments.

Now *be yourself*—whatever that means to you. Be yourself in such a way that you, and only you, are in an evaluative position. Forget about trying to please or accommodate anyone but yourself. Now deal with the following questions:

What and whom do *you* deem valuable?

How do you *want* to behave toward these persons and things?

How *do* you behave toward them?

Do you handle them with the care they deserve, in accordance with their value to you?

What does your life mean to you right now?

What *could* it mean to you—now and in the future?

What are you doing—in concrete behavioral terms—to make your life what it could be?

What do you want out of your life?

What are you doing to make that vision happen for you?

Now bring your PARENT and CHILD back into awareness.

Let them show themselves—whenever appropriate and productive—in a very natural, easy kind of way. But always be aware of them and the impact they are having on you.

AWARENESS 5

Attaining a personal integrity—that's what we're about here. *Integrity* literally means a *wholeness*—for our purposes, a wholeness of personality. We're talking about being completely human, completely alive. 100%.

But don't misunderstand. Having a wholeness of personality doesn't mean that your life will suddenly become carefree. It doesn't mean that you will never again be tired or angry or frustrated. Not at all! Wholeness of personality has to do with the intensity of your experience—tuning in completely to the various moments of your life, the bad times as well as the good.

Wholeness is daring to experience totally your being.

Coming into your own as a communicator

The Component Model and Transactional Analysis provide rich insights into the complex structure of the self. But understanding that structure is only the beginning in developing the ability to engage in authentic communication. We must come to a full and complete selfness if we are going to relate to ourselves and others in an authentic way.

Coming into your own as a communicator—becoming a whole and together person—is a growth process at the very heart of authentic communication. This growth process involves several steps:

Self-Awareness

Self-Assessment

Self-Direction

Self-Responsibility
Self-Actualization

Self-Actualization is where we want to *be*, because this is
the point at which we *become* whole and complete persons.
It should be noted that these various steps are not mutu-
ally exclusive. That is, one does not necessarily exclude—or
stand completely apart from—the other four. There is overlap between and among all of them. Movement in the direction of self-responsibility, for example, enhances self-
awareness, in that it serves to make more clear who I am in
my behaviors.

Recognizing the interplay between and among these
steps, let us go through them one at a time:

Self-Awareness

This is a matter of getting in touch with who I am at any
given moment in a relationship, being aware of my own self
in relation to another person. The whole person is keenly
aware of the various dimensions and nuances of his own self:
his strengths and weaknesses, his needs, his wants, his fears,
his anxieties, his joys, his dreams, his feelings. He evidences a
congruency—or internal balance—between who he is and
what he is doing and thinking and feeling at any given moment. He knows what he is about. And he owns up to it: He
claims ownership of his ideas, emotions, desires, and intentions. In a phrase, the whole person knows where he is at any
given moment.

Self-Assessment

The whole person is aware of who he is at any given
moment. But he does not necessarily like everything he sees.
And so he sets about assessing (or evaluating) himself in light

of his behaviors. (This self-assessment does not involve "getting down on" oneself. The focus of the evaluation is not so much the *self* as it is *behavior*.)

Self-assessment is a critical awareness of the self—and then some, in that it involves a critical estimation of who I am as I reveal myself in my behaviors. The whole person does not accept as efficacious every one of his behaviors; he would never say, "Well, that's just the way I am." Rather, he understands that he must evaluate those behaviors and ask, "Is this who I want to be and is that the way in which I want to behave?"

Self-assessment concerns itself with the productivity or non-productivity of certain behaviors. It asks whether this or that behavior is productive or counterproductive, whether this or that behavior is conducive to continued self-growth. If the behavior is productive, it is retained. But if it is counterproductive, it is recognized as such and is systematically eliminated.

Self-assessment is not an undue preoccupation with one's own self; it is a necessary part of developing one's own personhood. It is an important moment in the continuing process of growing up emotionally.

Self-Direction

The whole person is a "self starter" in that he determines the course of his own destiny. He refuses to allow himself to be determined or defeated by external circumstances. This does not mean that he remains unaffected by persons or events—that would be neither possible nor desirable. The whole person is active and involved—a doer—and necessarily is touched by all kinds of happenings. But these extraneous things do not deter him from pursuing his own growth-agenda.

The self-directing person is open to things outside him-

self. In fact, he goes out toward his environment, recognizing
that it contains a wealth of beauty and joy. But this "going out
toward" is always done freely; there is no compulsive need to
please others or to become what they want him to be. The
environment (and its mood) does not change the self-
directing person. Rather he changes it, imprinting on it his
own special mark and influencing it for the better.

The alternative to self-direction is surrender: giving
oneself up to the whims and fancies of external circumstance. The surrender itself sounds something like this:

"She made me so mad. . . ."

   or

"He won't let me do anything. . . ."

   or

"If only it weren't for. . . ."

These are the voices of *other direction*, a frame of mind in
which we are controlled (and often crippled) by persons and
events outside ourselves. These outside voices tell me that
other things make me who I am, and that simply is not (or at
least does not have to be) true. *I am of my own making.* And the
sooner I realize that, the more fully human I will become.

Self-Responsibility

This is very closely related to self-direction. In fact, the
one follows quite naturally from the other. The self-directing
person quite properly recognizes himself as an *actor*, not a
reactor: He moves out from himself toward others in a very
relaxed, unhurried, and nonpressured kind of way. Because
he acts (instead of simply reacting to external circumstances),
the whole person is in a position to assume responsibility for
his behaviors.

The fully human person does not waste energy wringing his hands, commiserating about how "unfair" life is or how "lousy" people are. He recognizes that, ultimately, his own behavior is his choice. External circumstances may push him in a certain direction, to be sure. But he realizes that, when all is said and done, he chooses to behave in this or that way.

This is a very important awareness, one that may sound strange at first hearing. Many of us unfortunately are in the habit of thinking that other persons and external circumstances work us over and, in the process, determine our behavioral responses. But, in reality, *all behavior is choice*. We choose the ways in which we will respond to various stimuli. Take *anger*, for example. Imagine this commonplace situation in which another person "makes" you angry: You are in a restaurant, relaxed and looking forward to an enjoyable dinner; you are feeling good and your behavior shows it. You study the menu and place your order in a cheerful, friendly kind of way. But the waiter is gruff and crabby, to the point of being downright discourteous. After several minutes of this kind of service, you find your mood suddenly changing. You become angry because of the waiter's attitude. You bark back at him and—what is worse—become short with your dinner companion. You become quiet and sullen, fuming inside and out. At these prices, you figure, you could at least expect civility from the waiter. And so that night's dinner is ruined for you and your companion. Not only is the evening spoiled, but, to add insult to injury, you leave with a beauty of an upset stomach.

What has happened here? You may argue that it was perfectly "normal" for you to have become angry with the rudeness of the waiter. "After all," you may argue, "he *made* me mad!" But that is not the point. We would do well to stop talking about "normalcy" and begin concerning ourselves with "productivity." How *productive* was your behavior? Was it *good for you* to have responded in that way? Did it help you to enjoy yourself that evening?

I am not suggesting that, in the example just cited, there is not an impulse to the emotion of anger. Nor am I suggesting that we should repress that emotion by refusing to recognize either its presence or its cause. But acting on that impulse and giving in to it in spite of its negative consequences—that is something else again. It comes down to this: In any given situation, it is incumbent on us (as fully human, functioning persons) to listen to our emotions and to hear their promptings. Then it is a matter of choosing those responses that are most productive for us and most in accord with our growth-plans. Pursuing our growth-plan in an aware way—that is what self-responsibility is all about.

Self-Actualization

This is the goal, the end toward which we must be moving if we are to become all that we can be as persons. The notion of self-actualization was first made popular by Abraham Maslow's delineation of a so-called "hierarchy of human needs." This hierarchy is shown in Figure 16.

Maslow says that we move from satisfying the most basic needs of survival to satisfying the more complex needs that relate to our emotional growth and development. But not everyone gets there. Some persons are fixated at the lowest two levels of satisfaction: They provide for their own safety and security, but go no further.

Moving in the direction of self-actualization is a choice a person makes. It is not something he needs from without, but something he craves from within. The movement toward self-actualization is motivated by the desire for continued emotional growth, rather than by some physiological deficiency.

It all goes back to the idea of *vision*: What do I want out

Figure 16

SELF-ACTUALIZATION - those needs that have to do with personal, human growth. Self-actualization allows one to be a fully alive and functioning person.

ESTEEM - those needs that have to do with maintaining respect - in my own eyes and in the eyes of others. This esteem involves my liking myself and being admired and looked up to by others.

LOVE AND BELONGING - those needs that have to do with being a part of something. This includes a wide range of human experiences: parental love and nurturing, friendship, romantic love, intimacy, and so on.

SAFETY - those needs that have to do with maintaining a total organismic protection from external threat. This includes physical security, as well as financial and emotional security.

PHYSIOLOGY - those needs that have to do with the most fundamental aspects of human survival: food, water, oxygen, shelter, sensory stimulation, and so on.

of life? And what does it mean to *be somebody?* Is it simply a
matter of amassing huge amounts of money, of collecting all
kinds of shiny material things? Is it a matter of having a fancy
executive title, of having other people bow and scrape at
your slightest whim? Or is there something more? Is becoming somebody a process that has to do with what you are
as a person inside? I think that it is. Becoming somebody is
self-actualization: It is a matter of becoming all the person
you can be. It is a matter of developing your human potential.

The self-actualizing person is never "finished," but
rather is in a continuing state of personal growth and mat-
uration. He is always moving, ever in the direction of enhancing his own personness. He is open to all that is happening
around him and drinks in each and every experience, wel-
coming it as an important dimension of his being. He is
keenly aware of his feelings and emotions, but is not vic-
timized or enslaved by them. He is able to give of himself
because he knows who he is and where he is going. He is able
to reach out for the strength and insight of others because he
knows that he participates in a collective humanity and that
he needs the sustenance others can provide. But this is never
a taking thing; it is always a genuine sharing of the human
adventure.

I am reminded here of a poster I saw in a bookstore
recently. It read something like this: "Love is always going
out from yourself toward others." Well, the sentiment is true
enough, as far as it goes. But it certainly does not say all there
is to say about the experience of human love. I would amend
the statement like this: "Love is always going out from yourself toward others . . . without ever leaving yourself behind."
In other words, the fully human person *gives of himself* in a
genuinely loving relationship, but he does not *surrender himself.* He does not give himself up in the relationship. If he

were to surrender himself, then he would not be able to contribute to the growth of the relationship as it evolves over time. The persons in any relationship must be concerned with one another, to be sure. But they also must be concerned with themselves as individuals; with their own personal growth. Only then will they be able to sustain the relationship over a period of time.

Self-actualization is not something that happens all of a sudden. You do not just awaken one morning, only to look in the mirror and see a self-actualized person (admittedly bleary-eyed) staring back at you. Self-actualization is something you make happen—a little bit at a time—with a lot of effort and a little help from your friends.

The process of moving toward self-actualization works like this: The self-actualizing person has a feeling for who he is right now and a vision of what he wants to become. He works out for himself a growth-plan to help him to realize that inner vision.

He continually monitors his own life experience, listening to the promptings that tug at him from within and attending to the urgings of his fellow men. He then integrates these, striking a balance that will allow him to be responsive to others and, at the same time, true to himself.

He does not automatically accept as appropriate or helpful every one of his behaviors, but, rather, "sees" himself and "listens" to himself as he interacts with others. Generally he knows what he is doing and why. And when he does not know the "hows" and "whys" of his behavior, he finds out.

Perhaps more than anything else, the self-actualizing person acknowledges and readily accepts the fact that he alone bears the ultimate responsibility for the way in which he handles himself in his interpersonal relationships. He sees himself as an actor, a person who makes value-choices and then carries out those choices in observable behavior.

AWARENESS 6

Love is not the issue here. Not really. You see, love is too mysterious. Why does my stomach do that funny little flip when I see her on the street? Why this one person, from among so many others? No, that feeling which we call *love* is just too hard for me to fathom.

The issue is the *relationship:* what we do with one another, how we treat one another, how we speak with one another, how we listen to one another. These are the things on which we must focus our energies. Love simply happens. But the relationship is something the two of us must make happen for ourselves. And it takes hard work. And lots of patience. And sensitivity. And. . . .

The experiences
of human communication

People come to one another through their communication.
We reveal ourselves to ourselves and to one another insofar
as we engage in the give and take of communication. It is not
an overstatement to insist that the human experience is
essentially a communication experience.

Speak that I may see you

Listen and you will see me

To be in the world in the company of other people is to
be there communicating. We simply cannot not send and
receive messages: Even in your silence you are sending me a

wealth of information; you are telling me all kinds of things. But there are several ways in which we can accomplish the communication that lies at the very heart of the human experience. There are several modes or varieties of communication. These different communication-types are shown in Figure 17 below.

The hierarchical presentation of these varieties of communication is intentional: There are important qualitative differences among the three. *Dialogue* stands at the highest level in that it is the most genuine and authentic of all communication experiences. But we are getting ahead of ourselves. Let us go through each of the communication types, one at a time.

At the lowest, most mundane level there is *Conversation*. Conversation is roughly analogous to phatic communication, in that it is the stuff of everyday, commonplace social experience. The bus stop, the dentist's office, the dinner party: These places are all buzzing with an almost endless stream of conversation. In fact, conversation seems to be everywhere in our society, given over as it is to an almost obsessive concern for getting along. The absence of conversation makes most of us uncomfortable. For example, how do we indicate that we are ill-at-ease in the company of someone else? We might say something like, "I couldn't think of a thing to say!" It is as though we feel a compulsive need to fabricate some kind of message to exchange with the other person—we even talk about "making" conversation. The explanation for this compulsive talking is simple enough: The other person has invaded our territory (our life-space), and this can be very threatening. Suddenly he is there, close enough to touch. We want to frisk him to see if he is friendly; to reassure ourselves of his friendly intentions. And the only socially acceptable way of doing this is to engage him in conversation, to disarm him and restore our territorial balance. In conversation we are feeling out one another verbally.

In and of itself, there is nothing wrong with conversation. It is not, however, a very significant kind of communication. Ultimately conversation is shallow and unsatisfying. There is no real investment in conversation—by either person. Nothing is ventured and, predictably, nothing is gained. It is all very pleasant and safe and antiseptic. And, as a result, our attention can be diverted and we can walk away from the other person without ever giving him or his message a second thought.

In a curious, almost paradoxical way, both persons in conversation remain loners. Each remains isolated from the other, as though imprisoned within the narrow confines of his own self. Each person can retain his own pretense and facade.

At a higher, more meaningful level, there is *Discussion*. Conversation is loose enough and free enough to deal with all kinds of subjects at once (in an admittedly superficial way). Not so discussion. Discussion, by definition, is a focused communication exchange that deals with a specific issue in a fairly in-depth way. Discussion is always purposive; it always aims at some end, even if the end is simply to exchange views on a particular subject.

Discussion is a higher type of communication than conversation, because in discussion I am sharing something of myself with you. I am making manifest my ideas, thoughts, and judgments—and you are responding in kind.

But discussion can still be a very "safe" kind of communication, because it is an intellectual thing. Discussion takes place in the head and not in the stomach. Discussion involves thoughts, not feelings; ideas, not emotions. Much discussion really is a kind of intellectual gamesmanship, in that, in many instances, it involves dealing with abstractions. For example, it is possible to discuss war without either person in the discussion really appreciating the horrors of that awful conflict. The discussion—heated though it may be—can be dispassionate because it remains a kind of "head game." It is *removed* from the reality which is being discussed.

At the highest, most meaningful level, there is *Dialogue*. Dialogue is the loftiest, most genuine, and authentic of all human communication experiences. It is also the most demanding and, accordingly, the most difficult to accomplish. Dialogue is open to the other person, and responsive to him, as well. Dialogue is patient and sensitive and caring. It is up-front, but never brutal, in its honesty; and it makes for an atmosphere wherein the other person can manifest the same kind of honesty. In sum, speaking dialogue is what being fully a person is all about.

We will consider dialogue in two different (but related) contexts: as a means of being with other people in general, and as a means of being with an intimate.

DIALOGUE AS A MEANS OF BEING WITH OTHER PEOPLE IN GENERAL

Being There Too

I am afraid that many of us regard other persons as though they simply were there too—in addition to us. We bump into one another (literally as well as figuratively) but do not *really see* one another. We do not recognize and acknowledge the uniqueness of the individual person, but, instead, merely consider others as though they were interchangeable parts in some kind of grand machine. We reduce everyone to the same plane and deal with them as though they were all the same. This kind of attitude makes life very simple and uncomplicated; we can formulate stock or standard behaviors and then merely plug these behaviors into any given situation. But—try as we might—we cannot forever deny the amazing complexity of the human experience. The sooner we admit that complexity (and act accordingly), the more satisfying our interpersonal relationships will be.

When I consider you as simply there too, you are beside me but have no real and discernible effect on me. It is as though we were living on a kind of huge subway train: bodies (not *persons*, but *bodies*) are pressed together, one next to the others. But we never really touch one another—our thoughts are our own; our feelings are very private; our facial expressions are blank and unchanging. In sum, we remain very much alone, even in the midst of the crowd.

Being With

Really being with somebody is a very different kind of experience. When I am *really with* another person, I recognize him as a unique, individual person. He and I are no longer merely in close physical proximity to one another; we are *together* in a shared, communal kind of experience.

Being with another person involves a *mutual presence*. We are present to one another: involved, committed, interested, fully attentive. I am really with you when my focus is fully on you, in this moment of our interaction.

The French philosopher, Emmanuel Levinas, deals with this notion of presence when he talks about the epiphany (or

appearance) of the *face*. He argues that our speaking is
ethical—fully a human event—only when the speaker recognizes and acknowledges the individual face of his partner in
communication. My communication with you is authentic
only when I see you as a person and acknowledge you as
such.

THE SPEAKING OF I–THOU

The Jewish philosopher, Martin Buber, was passionately
concerned with discerning ways in which people can come to
one another in communication that is fully human and authentic. Buber delineated two fundamental attitudes that we
can maintain in our dealings with other persons: *I–Thou* and
I–It.

In the I–Thou relationship, I not only recognize you as a
unique, fully functioning individual, I respect you as such
and refuse to trample on or do violence to your individuality.
I speak my thoughts and feelings in an honest and open
way—candidly and without pulling any punches because I
want to give you the gift of myself. But I do not impose these
thoughts and feelings on you. I refuse to insist that they
become your thoughts and feelings. I do not seek to put
limits on you by asking you to become merely a mirror image
of me. I allow you your own autonomy as a person and guard
that autonomy just as jealously as I guard my own.

The relationship of I–Thou: This is what dialogue is all
about. I speak so that I can tell you who I am. And I listen—
fully tuned-in and attentive—so that you can tell me who you
are. We meet one another in the Thou-saying as we really
are—without sham, pretense, and false sophistication.

In the I-Thou relationship, I love people and use things

The I–It relationship is something quite different from the experience of I–Thou. Buber himself talks about the I–It relationship as one characterized by what he calls "experience and using." His characterization is very much on-target. In the I–It relationship, I regard you as an object, as a thing, merely there for my design and manipulation. I use you for my own selfish purpose—until you are used up and, therefore, no longer valuable as an asset; at that point, I terminate the relationship (such as it was) and discard you.

Needless to say, the I–It relationship is a crippling, dehumanizing experience. But I am afraid that our culture is conducive to this kind of relationship: Competition, not cooperation, seems to be the order of the day. All too often we regard ourselves and others as objects of barter. We are in the habit of manipulating one another in order to accomplish our own selfish ends.

In the I-It relationship, I love things and use people

With these concepts in mind, then, we can come to an understanding and appreciation of what dialogue is all about. And we can also see the pitfalls of its counter-experience—monologue:

Dialogue demands
"Being With"
Presence
The Speaking of I–Thou

Monologue is resigned to
"Being There Too"
Non-Presence
The Speaking of I–It

Think of it as though interpersonal communication takes place on a kind of continuum: On the one extreme there is monologue and, on the other, dialogue. There are gradations all along the way (see Figure 18), indicating that we move increasingly in the direction of dialogue as we grow as persons.

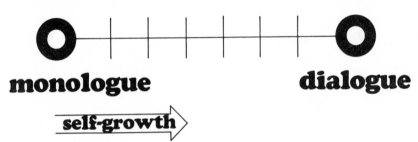

Figure 18

AWARENESS 7

For young marrieds and other lovers: What about our relationship? Are we really touching one another or are we simply living together? There is a big difference between the two. People who just live together are like calves in a storm—they huddle close to one another because they are afraid of the noise and commotion around them. Their being together is motivated by fear.

But people who touch one another—how very different and how much grander that is! They reach out to and embrace one another because they want to share the full experience and expression of their humanness. Their sharing is motivated by love.

All real love is touching. Not just sexual touching (as adolescents believe), but mental and emotional touching as well.

Monologue

The kind of monologue to which we are referring here is not a soliloquy in the normal sense of that word. It is not something that takes place on the stage, with an actor or actress addressing the audience. In monologue as we are talking about it, another person is there in the communication exchange—but only there too.

Researchers tell us that children speak six times more in the presence of others than they do when they are alone. The mere physical closeness of another person seems to stimulate them and sets them to talking. But this compulsive chatter is not necessarily meaningful conversation. Children are notorious for pursuing their own individual communicative agenda, even in the physical presence of other people.

Many adults (who have matured physically, but not emotionally) exhibit the same kind of childish communicative behavior. And this is what monologue is all about. In monologue, each person in the interaction pursues his own agenda. Each uses the other as a "message receptacle."

Dialogue

This is a kind of communication style characterized, above all, by *reciprocity*. It is truly and completely an exchange of meanings. Neither person in the dialogue forces the issue by pursuing his own particular agenda. Rather, each adapts his style so as to accommodate their mutual, shared needs.

Do not misunderstand all of this: Dialogue is not necessarily a completely pacific, tranquil, idyllic kind of coexistence. It does not mean a complete harmony or absolute agreement. In fact, the real test of dialogue comes when the partners are in disagreement about the issues at hand: Even when disagreeing about specific points, can we still respect one another's viewpoints? Can I allow you your own thoughts and feelings, or do I resent your independent spirit? **Dialogue is not persuasion. It is a sharing of who we are, what we think, and how we feel.**

At the bottom line, dialogue is an *attitude* the partners in communication manifest toward one another. The special virtue of the partners in dialogue is *empathy*—the ability to feel along with one another. In dialogue, each partner wants only to understand the other as completely as he can; to be able to say, without reservation, "I hear you. I share your feeling. I am feeling it with you." In order to accomplish this empathy, each partner must make himself accessible to the other: He must step out from the narrow confines of his own personal world-view and see things as the other person sees them. **The aim of dialogue is an understanding and appreciation of one another. Neither person seeks to conquer or to victimize the other.**

In his book, *The Miracle of Dialogue*, theologian Reuel Howe notes this healing dimension of dialogue: "Every man is a potential adversary, even those whom we love. Only through dialogue are we saved from this enmity toward one another."[1]

Martin Buber is insistent in his admonition that dialogue is a very special kind of communication experience, one that is difficult to come to, but the key to the continued well-being of humanity itself. He cautions us lest we become so caught-up in the busyness of everyday living that we lose sight of (and touch with) the higher reality of our common human experience:

> Hearkening to the human voice, where it speaks unfalsified, and replying to it, this above all is needed today. The busy noise of the hour must no longer drown out the *vox humana*, the essence of the human which has become a voice. This voice must not only be listened to, it must be answered and led out of the lonely monologue into the awakening dialogue of

[1]Reuel Howe, *The Miracle of Dialogue* (New York: Seabury Press, 1963), p. 3.

the peoples. Peoples must engage in talk with one another through their truly human men if the great peace is to appear and the devastated life of the earth renew itself.[2]

Buber recognizes that the human task—a task each person must assume for himself—is to develop our inherent potentialities. He refers to this development as the "realization of man." People "realize" themselves (and actualize their human resources) insofar as they rise above the petty meanness that marks so much of everyday conversation, insofar as they transcend the mundane discourse (the empty words and trite phrases) that plague so many of our interactions. Witness Buber's eloquent and impassioned plea:

> The name Satan means in Hebrew the hinderer. That is the correct designation for the anti-human in individuals and in the human race. Let us not allow this Satanic element in men to hinder us from realizing man! Let us release speech from its ban! Let us dare, despite all, to trust![3]

DIALOGUE: WHAT IS NECESSARY

In very general terms, dialogue demands a fullness of person of each of the participants in the encounter. But this fullness is always a "process" experience. That is, no one of us can ever expect (or even hope) to be done in terms of individual growth. The aim, rather, is to be on the way, to be in a state of *becoming*.

More specifically, the experience of dialogue involves the following elements:

[2,3]These quotations are from the essay, "Genuine Dialogue," by Martin Buber. The essay can be found in a number of texts.

1. An in-depth understanding of the self
2. An in-depth understanding of the other
3. Explicit message sending—there is no room in dialogue for ambiguity and hidden agenda (an ulterior motivation that prompts a given message)
4. A deep and abiding trust of the self
5. A deep and abiding trust of the other
6. Empathic and active listening

These elements of the experience of dialogue constitute a kind of "carousel dynamic," as shown in Figure 19. The person who earnestly seeks out the experience of dialogue can "get on" the carousel at any given point. He will then get caught up in the internal dynamic of dialogue and will proceed to move through the cycle. The important thing is to get on, to get going and begin the process. **The life of dialogue is a self-perpetuating process: The more you engage in dialogue, the easier it becomes.**

The carousel works like this: My understanding of my own self helps me to fathom my thoughts and feelings and to take responsibility for them. I then can begin to break down my defense mechanisms and to behave as I "really" am in that particular moment. When I know myself and accept myself, then I am in a position to get to know you as you "really" are.

My increased understanding of you helps me to appreciate your joys, anxieties, values, attitudes, and perceptions. Because I understand you—as you really are—I want to set about having a deep and meaningful relationship with you. In order to make this relationship happen, I become increasingly explicit in my messages: I say what I mean, and I mean what I say.

When I hear myself speaking what I really mean to say, then I am well on the way toward cutting through the trite-

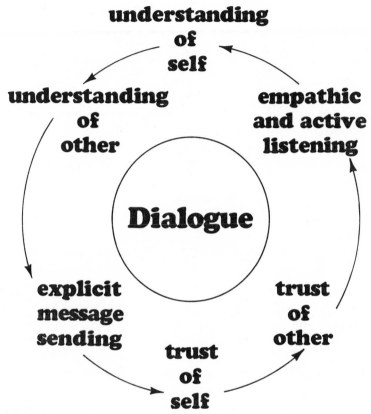

Figure 19

ness and game-playing that previously had plagued my communications. When I am no longer playing games with myself, then I can come increasingly to trust myself and my judgments and my emotions.

When I trust myself and my judgments and my emotions, then I am able to rely on the rightness of my positive feelings for you. I like you and want to get to know you even better as a person. And so I have confidence and trust in you as a partner in our shared human experience.

When I trust you as a person and my defense mechanisms are no longer in the way, then I can really hear what you are *meaning* and not just what you are saying. I invite your confidences, and prove this by listening to you in an empathic and active way.

When I listen empathically and actively to your meanings, I not only hear what you are really saying; I also get valuable insights into the way in which you are perceiving me in the interaction. I get feedback about how I am coming across. And this feedback serves to enhance my understanding of myself.

And so the carousel keeps moving. The qualities that prompted the dialogue in the first place become ever stronger. And my partner and I keep growing in our individual and collective selves.

DIALOGUE AS A MEANS OF BEING WITH INTIMATES

Theoretically it is possible for a person to engage in dialogue with virtually everyone whom he meets. In terms of your everyday interactions, however, it is not always necessary. You may have neither the time nor the inclination nor the need to engage in this very special kind of encounter with the postman or the busdriver or the grocery clerk. Insofar as these dealings are concerned, civility and decency are probably quite enough.

But in the intimate relationship—in the one-to-one relationship of love—dialogue is not an option. It is an absolute necessity if the relationship is to prosper and to grow. **Dialogue is the language of intimacy**.

In his remarkable little book, *The Secret of Staying in Love*,

John Powell reminds us that the key to the loving relationship is communication.[4] The human experience of love has been likened to a germinating seed that pokes its tiny head through the ground and into the light of day. The seed contains within itself the possibility of blossoming into a growing, living thing of beauty. But if left unattended—if it is not nurtured and cared for—the seed will wither and die, its promise unrealized. So it is with love. Love happens in a mysterious way. We do not really understand how or why—it just happens to us. But the romantic blush that accompanies the onset of love will pale and eventually disappear unless the partners in the relationship take care of their love. Falling in love is something that happens to us. But staying in love— and letting our love prosper and mature—is something we must *do*. And this doing of love is what dialogue is all about.

> Love is . . . a high inducement to the individual to ripen, to become something in himself, to become world for another's sake. It is a great, an exorbitant demand upon him, something that chooses him out and calls him to vast things. . . . love consists in this, that two solitudes protect and touch and greet each other.[5]

To stand in this kind of love—to reach out and to embrace another person without reservation—is the most completely human of all communication experiences.

The dialogue of intimacy assumes all of the attributes already outlined in our consideration of dialogue. But, as you might expect, dialogue in the intimate relationship is more intense; more focused in its direction. **In the intimate relationship, dialogue is the sharing of feelings and emo-**

[4]John Powell, *The Secret of Staying in Love* (Niles, Ill.: Argus Communications, 1974).

[5]Rainer Maria Rilke, *Letters to a Young Poet*, trans. M.D. Herter Norton (New York: W.W. Norton & Company, Inc., 1954), pp. 54, 59.

tions. The intimate dialogue demands a continuing openness between partners, an openness that goes to the very core of their individual selves, their feelings.

DIALOGUE AND SELF-DISCLOSURE

When I genuinely love another person, I want to share myself with that person. Of course, we will share our thoughts on those commonplace affairs of everyday living: We will talk about the budget, the weather, where we want to go for vacation, and (when we are feeling especially catty) the neighbors across the street. But that will not be enough for us. We will want to go beyond this ordinary kind of discussion (important though it may be) to a deeper dialogue. And in order to accomplish this deeper dialogue, we will have to engage in *self-disclosure*.

When I disclose myself to you, I tell you who I really am. Not just what I think, but what I feel. In self-disclosure, I give you the greatest gift I can: myself. I cut through all the pretense and the defense mechanisms that have served as a buffer between us, and I let you meet the real me.

But self-disclosure is easier to talk about than it is to do. It is a terribly risky thing for me because I come to you with all my defenses put aside. I present myself to you just as I am—and you may not accept me; you may not understand me; you may even laugh at me. And that would hurt me deeply. And so, rather than risk that hurt, I may simply choose not to disclose myself. John Powell recognizes the risk in self-disclosure when he asks, "Why am I afraid to tell you who I am?" And he answers something like this: "I'm all I have. If I give myself over to you and you reject me, I won't have anything left."

So self-disclosure is a risky, chancy thing. But we must

learn to take the risk if we want our intimate relationships to be of high quality. **Self-disclosure is what intimacy is all about: You can never come to know me unless I tell you who I am.** Even more than that, some amount of self-disclosure seems to be absolutely necessary to a state of physical and emotional well-being. There is substantial research evidence to suggest that psychosomatic illness is the result of repressed emotions. We keep all of our anxieties and hurts and fears and angers bottled-up inside us, but this repression does not do anything to make these feelings go away. They find their outlet by eating away at the lining of the stomach, resulting in ulcers; or they cause migraine headaches; or insomnia; or any one of a number of other psychosomatic ailments. (A note here: A psychosomatic illness is not imaginary at all. It is a very real illness with a very real pain. It is called "psychosomatic" because the root cause of the problem is an emotional conflict that remains unresolved. In dealing with this kind of illness, we must treat the whole person: We must pay attention to the emotional cause of the difficulty as well as the physical symptom.)

Self-disclosure seems to come especially hard in our culture, because we put such a premium on keeping up a front and appearance. Think about some of the commonplace stereotypes:

Big boys don't cry—we teach our men, from their earliest years, to *appear* strong and unbending, *in spite of* what they may be feeling. The end-result of this is the calculated denial of honest human emotions. Many men are afraid to show emotion because they have been conditioned to be suspicious of those emotions. They have been taught that they should somehow be above all that. But denying those emotions does not make them go away. It only gives us ulcers. Or worse. Sometimes these repressed feelings—allowed to fester for so long—finally erupt in a torrent of violent hostility.

Little girls are made of sugar and spice and everything nice—

we teach our women, from their earliest years, to *appear* sweet and demure and proper, *in spite of* what they may be feeling. Here, too, the end-result is the denial of honest human emotion. (This stereotype, of course, is being broken down at present, with the rise of the women's movement. But, as the women are finding out, old stereotypes die hard.)

There are many more examples of this kind of stereotyping. For example, we expect our priests and ministers somehow to be above all human foibles and imperfections. Granted these persons should set some kind of example for their parishoners. But we must allow them their humanness at the same time. Otherwise we put a great emotional pressure on them, a pressure that is hard to endure. They become afraid to admit their weaknesses and failings, even to themselves. And so they cannot confront these weaknesses and work on them in a constructive way.

Sometimes our fear of self-disclosure is rooted in a misunderstanding of the nature of human emotion. We simply must recognize the reality that all emotions are amoral. That is, an emotion cannot be adjudged either "good" or "bad." An emotion simply *is*. It exists and, therefore, is genuine and legitimate. There is no need to be afraid of any of our emotions. Our emotions and feelings make us most truly who and what we are. Our emotions and our feelings are what distinguish us as individuals from everybody else. While we need not fear our emotions, we must learn to pay attention to them and try to understand what prompts them.

Emotions are outside the realm of morality. But many of us make moral judgments about our emotions, with the result that we feel bad about feeling in a certain way. Many of us feel bad about feeling bad, and this is a crippling response to our emotions—we put ourselves into a real bind. We simply cannot help feeling what we feel.

Now, of course, there is a difference between *feeling* an emotion and *acting on* that emotion. When we talk about *acting*, then we get into the realm of moral judgments. We must recognize that some actions are productive, but some are counterproductive; some are responsible, but some are irresponsible. But when we judge the emotions themselves, we can become immobilized. We think that there must be something wrong with us for feeling this or that emotion. And so we repress the emotion, which is the same as running away from it:

> *We never confront the emotion so as to learn what prompts it.*
>
> *We never confront the emotion so as to decide whether to act on it.*
>
> *We never confront the emotion so as to learn more about ourselves.*

If you seriously want to improve your ability to engage in self-disclosure, you must face up to your own emotions: Recognize them, admit them, study them, listen to them, and understand them. Then and only then can you decide whether it is productive for you to act upon them in this particular instance.

THE LANGUAGE OF INTIMACY: HOW TO SPEAK IT

The speaking of intimate dialogue is a three-part process:

1. You begin by telling your partner what you are feeling. For example:

"I am tired. . . ."

"I am anxious. . . ."

"I am happy. . . ."

"I am angry. . . ."

2. Then you continue to elaborate on that feeling by telling your partner as best you can what prompted this feeling. For example:

> "I am tired because I only got four hours of sleep last night."
>
> "I am anxious because I am not sure that you still love me."
>
> "I am happy because we were able to be together tonight."
>
> "I am angry because you were thirty minutes late."

3. And then you elaborate still more on what you are feeling, with the intention of making yourself transparent to your partner. Open yourself as completely and as honestly as you can. And then let your partner respond just as completely and as honestly as he or she can.

This process may seem very simple and, perhaps, too easy to be worthwhile. Well, it is simple. But it is not as easy as it may seem. This kind of dialogue can only work when there are two persons who are committed to doing whatever is necessary to enhance the quality of their relationship. Their focus must always be on the relationship—and on ways to improve it.

This kind of intimate dialogue demands:

1. That neither person judge the other—if you perceive me as judgmental and evaluative about what you are feeling, then you will become silent; you will be reluctant to be completely open with me.

2. That neither person speak for the other—the partners in dialogue must be careful only to speak for themselves. You may tell me how you are *perceiving* me; in fact, this is important to the dialogue. But do not tell me *why* I am

doing this or that; do not tell me what I am feeling. Speak only what you are feeling and thinking. And then invite me to respond for myself.

Check yourself out and see how often this formula for dialogue would be useful in your own intimate relationships. Take this very commonplace example:

A man picks up his fiancée for dinner. She senses right away that there is something wrong, that something is bothering him. She continues with what becomes more and more a one-sided conversation, until she begins to get angry. Exasperated, she finally asks, "What's wrong with you?" He continues to stare straight ahead and responds, "Nothing." Meanwhile he tightens his grip on the steering wheel. She comes back with, "Don't tell me that nothing's wrong. Are you mad at me?" He snaps, "I told you that nothing is wrong. Let's just drop it." And she snaps right back, "OK! OK! I'm sorry I asked!" And they sit in silence. A perfectly good evening is now well on its way toward becoming perfectly miserable.

Sound familiar? Probably so. This kind of interaction happens all the time in relationships. But it is so harmful and disruptive. And so unnecessary. Imagine all the energy wasted in this particular interaction.

Speaking the language of intimacy requires energy too. And effort and patience and caring. Perhaps most of all caring. But it is worth that energy because it works.

AWARENESS 8

What to do till the doctor comes—an ℞ for ailing relationships: Don't talk. At least not yet. Listen. To yourselves and to each other. And then report what you've heard.

AFTERWORD

Final thoughts

And so that is our exploration of the workings of human communication. Did you learn anything? Do you know any more about communication now than you did when we began? I cannot test you on these questions by asking you to recite for me. Nor would I want to. Your interpersonal behavior is the only real test of what you have learned: If you learned anything, it will show itself in your behavior; you will handle yourself differently in your dealings with other people. The various situations in which you find yourself everyday will serve as the proving grounds for your insight into the dynamics of human communication.

I am convinced that the study of human communication is a very serious business. After all, we play out our lives—for better or worse—in an arena of interpersonal communication. To be sure, we often take that communication for granted. But this does not diminish the importance of communication in our lives; it merely points up our own lack of understanding of what it is to be fully human.

The fully human person is tuned into himself in his relationships with other people. And he recognizes that the relationships in which he is involved turn on communication: The relationships themselves can be no better or worse than the communication that characterizes the relationships. In other words, the relationships rise or fall on the kind of communication patterns that the partners work out with one another.

But what of this communication? What about the speaking in which we engage? Indeed, speech is a miracle. It is also a mystery. Our sophisticated diagnostic tools notwithstanding, no one completely understands just exactly how speech works or even what it is. But we do know this: Speech is not merely an organismic function, but rather a function of the mind and the spirit.

In point of fact, there is no single anatomical locus for the act of human speaking. We speak with the voice box, but only because we have certain cerebral structures as well. The larynx, the lungs, the tongue, the mouth—these all must work in conjunction with one another to make speech happen. (Even the hearing mechanism comes into play here, as is evidenced by the fact that the person who is deaf from birth requires special help to develop some speech abilities.)

People experience their own speech as a *possibility*. That is, speech contains within itself the possibility of enhancing the quality of human life in general and the character of an individual life in particular. The Jesuit scholar, Father Walter Ong, comments on this "possibility" dimension of speech as follows:

What words do is precisely annihilate the in-betweenness which separates you from me and me from you. When I speak to you, I am inviting you to enter into my consciousness, and I am entering into yours. When you listen to me, you pretend that you are saying the same things I say to find whether they make sense. When I speak, I listen to myself to see if I am making sense to you. The listener speaks while the speaker listens. Words are invitations to community, to sharing. . . .[1]

But many times the lofty possibility of speech remains unrealized. Increasingly in our consumer-oriented culture, speech is not deemed a possibility, but, rather, a *currency*. Speech has become a medium of barter and exchange. For example, the notion of "image" (a notion that pervades virtually every facet of our culture—politics, fashion, and so on points up the fact that we are more interested in appearance than substance, more concerned with superficiality than authenticity. We use speech to sell ourselves and, as a result, we often sacrifice our genuine thoughts and feelings for the sake of social acceptance.

When we sell ourselves out, we also sell ourselves short; we surrender the vision that is essential to the realization of our individual and collective human potential. In the short run, the "image" person can attain success and prestige. But, in the longer run, he comes away empty and unfulfilled. Only authenticity (a state of being that shows itself in authentic speech) can bring about a condition of deep and abiding well-being.

One of the problems with speech is that it is malleable: People can shape their words in such a way as to make them

[1]This quotation is from the essay, "The Power and Mystery of Words," by Walter J. Ong, S.J., which appeared in *Saint Louis University Magazine*, vol. 45, no. 5, October 1972.

serve their own purposes. Consider, for example, the speech that attended the Watergate coverup: Lies became "inoperative statements"; a coordinated effort to subvert the democratic process became a "third-rate burglary"; and a press-release mentality tried to make a felonious conspiracy seem a simple error in judgment.

Indeed, people can shape their speech as they wish. But there comes a point at which their speech turns back on them and begins to shape them and the way in which they view the world. It is easy to call a lie an "inoperative statement." But what happens when we do? Even as we speak the phrase, the fundamental difference between right and wrong begins to blur. And before long we can no longer recognize falsehood or distinguish it from truth.

The reality is that speaking—like existence itself—imposes a burden on us: It forces us into interaction with one another and demands that we live with the results of that interaction. But, paradoxically, the burden is a welcome one, for it allows us to work through the difficulties of being human in such a way that we can find ourselves in embracing others.

Authenticity does not promise an idyllic life free from pain, hurt, and disappointment. In fact, the authentic person—aware of himself in relation to others—may well feel anguish more deeply than other people. But his awareness is such that he knows that this is what it is to be human: to forego the false security of hiding himself behind pretense and facade and to take the risk of reaching out to others in an open, honest encounter. And so—even when he hurts—the authentic person celebrates the fact that he is fully alive and aware.

Freeing yourself to really experience life: This is what the study of human communication is all about. It is not an easy thing to do. But working at it in earnest is a heady, exhilarating experience. And once you have been there, you will never settle for anything less than being all the person you can be.

Good Luck. And get growing. *Now!*

Index

Adapted child, 78
Adult ego state, 76–80, 83, 87–88
Amplification, 40
Anger, 93–94
Anger stamps, 83
Assumptions, 63, 74, 84
Authentic communication, 5–6,
    55–119
  communion and, 57–60
  conversation, 100–101
  defined, 55
  dialogue, 100, 102–3, 105–19
  discussion, 100, 101–2
  self-actualization, 90, 94–97
  self-assessment, 89, 90–91

Authentic communication *(cont.)*
  self-awareness, 21–22, 89, 90
  self-direction, 89, 91–92
  self-disclosure, 114–17
  self-responsibility, 90, 92–94
  self-understanding *(see* Self-
    understanding)
Authentic communion, 60
Awareness principles, 6, 13–14,
    32–33, 48, 60, 88, 98, 106,
    119

Behavior, 74, 84
  defined, 64
Belief system, 41–43

Berne, Eric, 75
Brown stamps, 83
Buber, Martin, 104–5, 108–9

Career orientation, 28–29
Change, coping with, 22–23
Child ego state, 76–80, 83, 86–87
Chooser self, 64–66
Clarification, 39
Closed mind, 41–43
Communication:
    authentic (*see* Authentic communication)
    breakdown in, 3, 4, 29
    defined, 4
    effective (*see* Effective communication)
    phatic, 58, 100
Communion, 57–60
Competition, 105
Component model of the self, 69–74
Context, 15–20
Conversation, 100–101

Delayed gratification, 68–69
Description, 36–37
Dialogue, 100, 102–3, 105–19
Disbelief system, 41–43
Discussion, 100, 101–2

Effective communication, 3, 4, 11–52
    clarification and, 39
    description and, 36-37
    flexibility and, 40–43
    listening and, 44–48
    making it happen, 35–48
    model of process of, 11–23
    openness and, 40–43
    perception, 5, 26–36

Effective communication (*cont.*)
    personalization and, 38–39
    quantification and, 37–39
Ego states, 75–80, 83–88
Empathy, 108, 112
Empirical self, 70–74
Envy stamps, 83
Esteem needs, 95
Estrangement, 51–52

Feedback, 62–63, 112
Feedback loop, 13, 15, 17, 20
Feedforward loop, 15, 17, 20
Feelings, repression of, 83, 115–17
Flexibility, 40–43
Futility life position, 81

Games People Play (Berne), 75
Gold stamps, 83
Gratification, delayed, 68–69

Howe, Reuel, 108

I, 14–15, 17, 20
Ibsen, Henrik, 64
I-It relationship, 105
I'm not OK-You're not OK, 81
I'm not OK-You're OK, 81
I'm OK-You're not OK, 80–81
I'm OK-You're OK, 80
Inferences, 63–64, 74, 84
Integrated adult, 79–80
Integrity, 88
Interruption, 47
Intimacy, 112–15, 117–19
Introjective life position, 81
I-Thou relationship, 104, 105

Jourard, Sidney, 67

Levinas, Emmanuel, 103–4

Life positions, 80–81
Life scripts, 81–82
Life-worlds, 15–16, 17, 20, 21, 28, 40
Listening, 44–48, 110, 111
Little Professor, 78
Love and belonging needs, 95

Maslow, Abraham, 94
Maternal deprivation syndrome, 82
Meaning, 12–13, 27
Medium, 13, 15, 17, 20
Message, 12–16, 41, 43
Metacommunication, 46, 48
Miracle of Dialogue, The (Howe), 108
Mirror self, 62–64, 65
Monologue, 105–7
Mutual presence, 103

Natural child, 78
Needs, hierarchy of, 94–95
Negative strokes, 82

Ong, Father Walter, 124–25
Onion self, 64, 65
Open mind, 41–43
Openness, 40–43
Other, 14–15, 17, 20, 110, 111
Other-alienation, 52

Parent ego state, 76–80, 83–87
Peer Gynt (Ibsen), 64
Penfield, Wilder, 75
Perception, 5, 16, 26–36
Perceptual ghosts, 29–32
Personalization, 38–39
Phatic communication, 58, 100
Phatic communion, 58–60
Physiology needs, 95
Pictured self, 70–73
Positive strokes, 82

Positive thinking, 32
Powell, John, 112–13, 114
Prejudgments, 47
Projected self, 70–74
Projective life position, 80–81
Psychosomatic illness, 115

Quantification, 37–38

Realization of man, 109
Responsibility, 60
Rokeach, Milton, 41
Roles and role-playing, 66-68

Safety needs, 95
Secret of Staying In Love, The (Powell), 112–13
Self, trust of, 110, 111
Self-actualization, 90, 94–97
Self-alienation, 51–52, 66
Self-assessment, 89, 90–91
Self-awareness, 21–22, 89, 90
Self-direction, 89, 91–92
Self-disclosure, 114–17
Self-fulfilling prophecy, 62–63
Self-growth, 22
Self-image, 29, 31, 32–33
Self-responsibility, 90, 92–94
Self-understanding, 61–88, 110–11
    chooser self, 64–66
    component model of the self, 69–74
    delayed gratification, 68–69
    mirror self, 62–64, 65
    onion self, 64, 65
    roles and role-playing, 66–68
    transactional analysis (*see* Transactional analysis)
Self-worth, 33
Sensitivity, 60
Shared meaning, 29, 30

Shared perception, 29
Silence, 4
Social environment, 15–20
Sound:
    giving of meaning to, 45–46
    reception of, 44–45
    recognition of, 45
Speaker, 12–15, 41, 43
Speech, 124–26
Stamps, 83
Stereotyping, 22, 115–16
Strokes, 82
Structural analysis, 74
Surrender, 92, 96–97
Survival needs, 94

Transactional Analysis (TA), 69,
        74–88
    ego states, 75–80, 83–88
    life positions, 80–81
    life scripts, 81–82
    stamps, 83
    strokes, 82

Unconscious projection, 47

Vision, 94, 96

Watergate, 126
Wholeness of personality, 88
Women's movement, 116